Managing Information Systems: Ten Essential Topics

Jun Xu

Southern Cross Business School, Southern Cross University
Gold Coast, Australia

Mohammed Quaddus

Graduate School of Business, Curtin University
Perth, Australia

AMSTERDAM – PARIS – BEIJING

Atlantis Press
8, square des Bouleaux
75019 Paris, France

For information on all Atlantis Press publications, visit our website at: *www.atlantis-press.com*

Copyright

This book, or any parts thereof, may not be reproduced for commercial purposes in any form or by any means, electronic or mechanical, including photocopying, recording or any information storage and retrieval system known or to be invented, without prior permission from the Publisher.

ISBNs
Print: 978-94-91216-88-6
E-Book: 978-94-91216-89-3

© 2013 ATLANTIS PRESS

Preface

Information systems have become an essential part and a major resource of the organization; and they can radically affect the structure of an organisation, the way it serves customers, and the way it helps people in the organization to communicate both internally and externally, and the way an organisation runs its business. Managing information systems effectively and efficiently has become an important part of the life of 21st century managers. This book is about managing information systems and focuses on relationships between information, information systems, people and business. The impacts, roles, risks, challenges as well as emerging trends of information systems are an important element of the book. At the same time, many strategic and contemporary uses of information systems such as implementing enterprise planning systems for improving internal operation, adopting customer relationship management systems and supply chain management systems to enhance relations with customers and suppliers/partners respectively, and establishing knowledge management systems for better managing organizational knowledge resources as well as using different information systems for supporting managers' decision making in all levels are an integral part of the book. In addition, essential and critical information systems management skills including using information systems for competitive advantages, planning and evaluating information systems, developing & implementing information systems, and managing information systems operation are a critical part of the book.

This book has ten chapters. Chapter 1 looks at foundations of information system/information technology and discusses topics such as the importance of information systems, key concepts of information systems, information systems competence for managers, critical issues of information systems, and emerging trends & future directions of information systems. In Chapter 2 an important dimension of managing information systems, how information systems can help organisations gain competitive advantages, is discussed.

Organisations can apply strategic planning tools such as Porter's five forces and value chain to analyse their competitive position, examine their competitive advantages, and identify relevant competitive strategies. Information systems can play a very important role in the success of an organisation's identified competitive strategies.

Chapter 3 studies the importance of good information systems planning, which is critical for the strategic use and success of information systems in the organization. Chapter 3 also looks at another important aspect of information systems management: evaluation of initiatives/investments of information systems. There is an old saying: 'If you cannot measure it, you cannot manage it'. Through systematic assessment of their information systems initiatives/investments, organizations can be effective in choosing right information systems projects and managing their chosen initiatives/investments. In order to measure the performance of information systems, organisations could use a set of metrics (such as net present value, return of investment, internal rate of return, payback period, and total cost of ownership)., Meanwhile organisations should look beyond financial metrics, and take into consideration of financial and non-financial data, qualitative and quantitative information, tangible and intangible costs/benefits, and formal and informal processes.

Chapter 4 looks at developing and implementing information systems. Correctly developed information systems can significantly contribute to the success of the business (i.e., enhancing competitive advantages, improving business performance). On the other hand, a poorly developed and implemented information system can have a damaging effect on business performance and can even cause a business to fail. To ensure successfully develop and implement information systems organizations need to adopt systems development life cycle (or its variations), which includes such activities as systems planning, analysis, design, development, testing, implementation, and maintenance. In addition, while organizations are developing and implementing information systems they have to pay close attention to such areas as project management, change management, and risk management, these areas are critically associated with the success of information systems development and implementation.

Chapter 5 discusses the importance of managing organization's knowledge resources/assets. Effectively managing and leveraging knowledge assets, has critical implications for business performance and sustainable business growth. Information systems such as knowledge management systems could assist in organization's efforts of capturing, storing, disseminating, utilizing and creating knowledge. On a related note, Chapter 5 also discusses data resources management. As a result of global connectedness, the wide adoption of computing tools & mobile devices, the rapid advancement of Internet technologies, and more powerful computing capability, gathering and analysing large (or large large) volume of data is quickly becoming popular among organizations for reasons such as better understanding customers, and better utilizing data resources & computing infrastructure.

Chapter 6 touches on the information systems infrastructure management and discusses hardware, software, networks and telecommunications management. Hardware is a vital part of computer systems and provides the underlying physical foundation for firms' information systems infrastructure. Other infrastructure components of software, networks and telecommunications require hardware for their storage and operation. To be useful, hardware needs software, which gives instructions that control the operation of a computer system. Networks and Telecommunications enable large and small businesses to communicate internally between staff and externally with customers, suppliers, business partners, strategic alliances and others. Making the right decision in relation to information systems infrastructure is vital to the success of the business.

Chapter 7 deals with functional information systems and discusses cross-functional information systems. Traditionally businesses are operated by dividing the organisation into various functions (i.e., accounting, marketing, finance, productions/operations management, human resources management) in a silo structure with each having its own information systems and tending to work in isolation. In order to deal with these problems of silo approach (i.e., information recreation, information errors, communication gaps among departments, loss of information arising from inaccurate information and not-timely shared information, and lack of consistent services to customers), managers need to think beyond the walls of the organisation. Thus there is a need for a cross-functional approach, which focuses on business process and customer services.

Cross-functional information systems are a strategic way to use information systems to share information resources and focus on accomplishing fundamental business processes in concert with the company's customer, supplier, partner, and employee stakeholders. Some typical examples of cross-functional information systems include: enterprise resource planning systems, customer relationship management systems, supply chain management systems, and knowledge management systems. These four systems have different focuses:

enterprise resource planning systems emphasize on internal efficiency; customer relationship management systems concentrate on customer relations; supply chain management systems focus on managing relations with suppliers and business partners; and knowledge management systems facilitate managing tacit and explicit knowledge of the organization. Meanwhile these four systems are inter-related (i.e., accurate information is critical to the success of supply chain management systems and enterprise planning systems; knowledge sharing facilitated by knowledge management systems is important to all the aspect of business including the success of supply chain management systems, enterprise planning systems, customer relationship management systems). Chapter 7 also has a close at enterprise planning systems and discusses implementation issues and emerging trends of enterprise resource planning systems. Chapter 8 looks at various aspects of customer relationship management systems and supply chain management systems, including benefits, types of systems/applications, challenges & issues of implementation, and future trends.

Chapter 9 reviews information systems for supporting decision making. Organisations today can no longer use a 'cook book' approach to decision making. In order to succeed in business today, companies need information systems that support the diverse decision-making needs of their operations. The massive volume of available data generated by billions of connected devices and human minds has further strengthened the role of information systems for decision-making support. Providing information and support for all levels of management decision making is no easy task. Therefore, information systems must be designed to produce a variety of information products to meet the changing needs of decision makers throughout an organisation. Examples of information systems for decision making cover management information systems, decision support systems, executive information systems, artificial intelligence applications, data warehousing & data mining, and business intelligence/business analytics.

Chapter 10 looks at managing information systems function and operation. The success of information systems in the organization heavily rely on good management. Good information systems management examines and works on enterprise information systems operation/function management, global information systems management, information systems in mergers and acquisitions, information skills & talent management, information systems governance, and global virtual team management. Chapter 10 also discusses information systems outsourcing management by looking at such areas as advantages and disadvantages of insourcing, outsourcing, and offshore-sourcing; critical capabilities, challenges, issues, and critical success factors of outsourcing.

We would like to thank Dr Chad Lin, Curtin University, Australia and Dr Daniel O'Sheedy, Photon Group, Australia, for their kind assistance in reviewing the book. Finally we would like to thank Atlantis Press and Springer for opportunity of working on the book, and thank Zeger Karssen, Publishing Director, Atlantis Press, for overseeing the publishing process of the book and for giving us such a wonderful publishing experience.

Jun Xu and Mohammed Quaddus
Gold Coast and Perth, Australia
November 2012

Contents

Preface   iii

1. Foundation   1

   1.1 Managing Information as a Strategic Resource 1
   1.2 Key Concepts of Information Systems 2
   1.3 Information Systems Competence for Managers 4
   1.4 Critical Issues of Information Systems Management 5
   1.5 Emerging Trends and Future Directions 13
   1.6 Summary 23
   Bibliography 24

2. Information Systems for Competitive Advantages   27

   2.1 Competitive Strategies 27
   2.2 Value chain 30
   2.3 Business Eco-systems and Co-opetition (Competition & Cooperation) . . 31
   2.4 Innovation Strategy 32
   2.5 Summary 38
   Bibliography 39

3. Information Systems Planning and Evaluation   41

   3.1 Strategic Alignment of Information Systems Plan with Business Strategy   41
   3.2 Measuring the Success of Information Systems Initiatives/Investments . . 45
   3.3 Financially Justifying Information Systems Investments 46

	3.4	Summary	50
		Bibliography	50
4.	**Developing and Implementing Information Systems**		**53**
	4.1	Systems Analysis and Design	53
	4.2	Project management, Change Management and Risk Management	58
	4.3	Internal Development, Outsourcing, Acquisition and Use of Application Service Providers	62
	4.4	Summary	65
		Bibliography	65
5.	**Managing Organization's Knowledge Resources**		**67**
	5.1	Data, Information and Knowledge	67
	5.2	Database, Data Warehouse and Data Mining	68
	5.3	The Phenomenon of Big Data	72
	5.4	Knowledge Management and Knowledge Management Systems	76
	5.5	Summary	80
		Bibliography	81
6.	**Managing Infrastructure for Information Systems**		**85**
	6.1	Hardware and Software Management	85
	6.2	Networks and Telecommunications Management	90
	6.3	Wireless Communication	93
	6.4	Management challenges	94
	6.5	Summary	106
		Bibliography	106
7.	**Using Information Systems for Enhancing Internal Operation**		**109**
	7.1	Functional and Cross-functional Information Systems	109
	7.2	Enterprise Resource Planning Systems	111
	7.3	Summary	118
		Bibliography	118

8. Using Information Systems for Improving External Relations — **121**

- 8.1 Customer Relationship Management Systems 121
- 8.2 Supply Chain Management Systems 131
- 8.3 Summary 136
- Bibliography 136

9. Using Information Systems for Supporting Decision Making — **139**

- 9.1 Enabling the Organization-Decision Making 139
- 9.2 Information Systems for Decision Support 141
- 9.3 Business Intelligence/Business Analytics 145
- 9.4 Management Challenges 147
- 9.5 Summary 148
- Bibliography 148

10. Information Systems Operation Management — **149**

- 10.1 Enterprise Information Systems Operation Management 149
- 10.2 Outsourcing 158
- 10.3 Global Information Systems Operation Management 162
- 10.4 Summary 164
- Bibliography 165

Chapter 1
Foundation

In this chapter, we will explain the importance of management of information resources, discuss the key concepts of information systems, explain information systems competence for managers, discuss critical issues of information systems, and discuss emerging trends and future directions of information systems.

1.1 Managing Information as a Strategic Resource

Efficient and strategic use of information holds the key to enhanced competitiveness, increased efficiency, better resource allocation, and improved effectiveness. Information resource is different with traditional tangible resources. Eaton and Bawden (1991) suggest some key distinctions between information as a resource and traditional tangible resources. They are:

- Value of information: it is difficult to quantify the value of information. For example, the same piece of information (i.e., information about the share price of Google) could lead to different impacts (positive or neutral or negative), and could have different values (small or large).
- Consumption of information: information has the characteristics of 'self-multiplicative', which basically says the information will not be lost or diminished when it is provided to others. This feature makes information resources fundamentally different with other (tangible and commodity) resources. For example, if I have a piece of information, I will still have it even after I share it with you; but if I have a tangible item (i.e., five dollars, one apple), if I share with others, then I won't have the same item (i.e., less than five dollars, not having the same whole apple I had before).
- Dynamics of information: information is a dynamic source for change. We need information to make changes and improve the way we do things. For example, by collecting

and analysing customer information, we can have better understanding customers' needs and concerns, thus are able to provide better products and services to customers.
- Life cycle of information: the life cycle of information is unpredictable; and information can have multiple life cycles. For example, how do you predict the information demand?; how do you predict the peaks and the troughs of information demand?; and how do you predict the declining and exit of information resources?. Information can be in one life cycle (being useful) then leaves (becoming irrelevant), but come back again in another life cycle later or enter other life cycles of information (for different stakeholders in different areas across various areas).
- Individuality of information: information has situational uniqueness. Information can come from different approaches (i.e., first-hand and second-hand information) and can exist various formats (i.e., digital and non-digital formats). Other tangible resources tend to have the identifiable format and sources (i.e., petroleum in liquid formats and coming from the underground or the bottom of the ocean).

1.2 Key Concepts of Information Systems

1.2.1 *The concept of information systems (IS)/information technology (IT)*

An information system includes all components and resources necessary to deliver information and information processing functions to the organisation and can be any organised combination of people, hardware, software, communication networks and data resources that collects, transforms and disseminates information within an organisation. Business professionals rely on many types of information systems that use a variety of information technologies, i.e. from simple manual (pen-and-pencil) hardware devices and informal (word-of-mouth) communication channels to complex computer-based systems (i.e. enterprise resource planning systems). However, in today's environment, when we talk about an information system, we refer to computer-based information systems, that use computer hardware and software, the Internet, and other telecommunication networks, and computer-based data resource management techniques to gather, manage and distribute information. The terms Information Technology (IT) and Information Systems (IS) will be used interchangeably in this book.

So far there is no universal classification of information systems applications. For example, information systems can be classified for the purpose of either serving business operations or supporting managerial decision making (O'Brien & Marakas 2011, p. 13).

On the other hand, information systems can be classified according to different needs at different organisational levels (i.e. strategic, management and operational levels) across various functions (i.e. sales and marketing, manufacturing and production, finance and accounting and human resources) (Laudon & Laudon 2005, p. 43). People at different levels of an organisation have different information needs. The structure of a typical organisation is similar to a pyramid. The array of organisational activities occurs at different levels of the pyramid. People in the organisation have unique information needs and thus require various sets of information systems tools. For example information systems such as management information systems, decision support systems, executive information systems, suit different information needs of operational managers, middle managers, and senior managers. Functional information systems, such as accounting information systems; finance information systems; marketing information systems; productions/operations information systems; and human resource information systems, serve different business functions.

Organisations are increasingly using cross-functional information systems, which focus on cross-functional business process and emphasize customer services. Examples of cross-functional information systems include enterprise resource planning systems, customer relationship management systems, supply chain management systems, and knowledge management systems.

1.2.2 *The concept of strategic information systems*

Strategic information systems are any kind of information systems that 'support or shape the competitive position and strategies of a business enterprise' (O'Brien & Marakas 2011, p. 46), and they play strategic roles and provide effective support in organisations' efforts for achieving competitive advantages (i.e. cost leadership, differentiation, innovation, growth, strategic alliance/partnership) (O'Brien & Marakas 2011, p. 49). Some examples of strategic applications of information systems include:

- use of enterprise resources planning systems for improving internal efficiency and effectiveness.
- use of customer relationship management systems for acquiring, enhancing and retaining customers and supply chain management applications for more effectively and efficiently managing supply chains.
- use of management information systems, decision support systems, executive information systems, and other information systems for decision support and better decision making.

- use of collaboration systems and knowledge management systems for better intra and inter-organisational collaboration and knowledge sharing.

1.3 Information Systems Competence for Managers

Information systems are a vital component for business success and a major functional area in business and therefore an essential field of study in many MBA programs. Information systems are an essential body of knowledge for business managers, professionals, and business students. As we argue information systems need to have a business view, business managers should participate in information systems decision-making for the following reasons (Pearlson & Saunders 2004, p. 3):

- Information systems have to be managed as a critical resource
- Information systems provide an opportunity to make changes in the way people work together
- Information systems work with almost every aspect of business
- Information systems create business opportunities and new strategies
- Information systems can assist in combating business challenges from competitors.

Based on a survey of information systems competence for MBA graduates among executives in 1995 (Ramakrishna *et al.* 1995), it is recommended that MBA graduates should equip themselves with such skills and knowledge as: general skills and knowledge of information systems, hardware skills, software skills, knowledge of applications, systems development, and knowledge of related topics including privacy, security, legal aspects, and ethical issues. The focus on soft skills (i.e., project management and information skills/talent management), is the trend identified in the survey. The same trend can be observed in today's business environment.

Meanwhile, business managers need to be able to discuss and examine the roles and consequences of information systems in the organization. Some dimensions and questions they should look at and ask include (Silver, *et al.* 1995, p. 376):

- What are an information system's features? What does it do?
- How does the information system match with the firm's external environment?
- How does the information system support the firm's strategy?
- How does the information system facilitate the firm's business processes?
- How does the information system work with the organisational structure and culture?

- Is the organisation's existing computing infrastructure suitable for the information system?
- Does the information system enhance the infrastructure? Does it extend it?
- How and how effectively was the system implemented?
- Who are the users of the system and how do they use it? as intended?
- What are the consequences of the information system for performance, people, and future flexibility? Did the system achieve its objectives?
- Do we want to use the information system to improve our business process or reengineer our business process?

1.4 Critical Issues of Information Systems Management

Organisations face various information systems management issues. Understanding these issues is very critical to the success of information systems in business. According to a recent study conducted by the Society of Information Management (SIM) in 2011, ten top IS/IT management concerns are (in the order): (1) IS/IT and business alignment; (2) Business agility and speed to market; (3) Business process re-engineering; (4) Business productivity and cost reduction; (5) IT strategic planning; (6) IS/IT reliability and efficiency; (7) Enterprise architecture; (8) Security and privacy; (9) Revenue-generating IS/IT innovations; and (10) IS/IT cost reduction (Luftman & Ben-Zvi, 2011). In the same study, top application and technology developments were also identified. Top ten application and technology developments include (in the order): (1) Business intelligence; (2) Cloud computing; (3) Enterprise resource planning systems; (4) Mobile and wireless applications; (5) Customer relationship management systems; (6) Software as a service; (7) Virtualization; (8) Collaborative and workflow tools; (9) Enterprise application integration/management; and (10) Data mining (Luftman & Ben-Zvi, 2011).

Meanwhile even though the key information systems management issues could be different for different organisations in different countries (i.e. arising from the differences in types of companies, industries, governments & regulations, IS/IT infrastructures, levels of sophistication, and cultures) and in different studies (i.e. resulting from differences in data collection methods, research subjects involved, and sample sizes), some common factors, which are basic to all businesses, can be identified: (1) focusing on customers; (2) building and enhancing relationships with business partners and suppliers; (3) fostering collaboration among people and teams across the organisation; and (4) improving operational efficiency and effectiveness; (5) enhancing business performance; (6) managing, developing and evaluating information systems; (7) protecting information resources; (8) using information systems ethically; and (9) managing information systems organisation.

In addition, according to one recent global survey of 1,469 senior executives of firms with different sizes and from different sectors and regions (reported in Brown & Sikes 2012), some challenges organizations faced for the success of digital technologies include:

- Organizational structure for successful deployment of digital technologies
- Lack of technology and information systems
- Lack of quality data
- Lack of internal leadership
- Difficulty in finding functional talent
- Inappropriate business processes to take advantages of opportunities created by digital technologies
- Lack of senior management support
- Difficulty in finding technical talent

1.4.1 *Management security & ethical issues*

Security and ethical implications of information systems is a must for strategic management and use of information systems. Even though they are only ranked Number 8 in the SIM 2011 survey, they are actually very critical issues for organizations and could cause serious damage financially to the organization (for example, according to RSA Anti-Fraud Command Center (reported in Enterprise Management Associates 2012), phishing attacks alone cost businesses US$ 1.3 billion in 2011). Organisations have to take them seriously; otherwise they may face the consequence of going out of business. Today's attackers are well organized and well informed, and they take advantages of latest advances in crimeware and hacking skills (Enterprise Management Associates 2012).

The global connectedness has made managing security and ethical issues a much more challenging task. Laseter & Johnson (2011) suggest that there are more than 5 billion devices connected to the Internet (a perpetrator needs only a single weakness in order to attack a system), accessing and serving up to 500 billion gigabytes of information and transmitting 2 trillion emails per day, furthermore 75% of emails are spam even though spam rate has been dropping in recent years. Every minute 42 new strains of malware (short for malicious software including viruses, worms, and Trojans) are generated, an average of 8,600 new websites with malicious code are developed each day, and half of the results for the top 100 daily search terms lead to malicious sites. Some major cyber technical attacks include: Malware, Unauthorized access, Denial of Services attack, Spam & Spyware, Hijacking (servers and pages), and Botnets (Turban *et al.* 2012, p. 500; Laudon & Laudon 2012, p. 246). And malware is number one cyber security concern. Another major issue is SPAM. Even though we do have solutions (i.e., Junk-mail filters, Automatic junk-mail deleters, Blocking certain URLs and e-mail addresses), it has been really challenging for controlling spamming since spammers send millions of e-mails, shifting Internet accounts to avoid detection and use different methods to find their victims.

Some attacks require sophisticated techniques and technologies, most attacks are not sophisticated (i.e., preying on poor security practice and human weaknesses), and insiders' breach could be more frequent and more harmful than that of outsiders. Effective security risk management procedures can be used to minimize their probability and impact. We as a society, which consists of individuals, institutions, businesses, and governments, need to work together to create an open but safe global community.

Effective security management of information technology is very critical to the success of a business. Security of today's networked enterprises is a major management challenge. Networked computer systems are highly vulnerable to various threats and failures, ranging from natural failure of hardware and software to misuse by information sysetms professionals and end users; and security weaknesses could be identified and explored in many parts of business operations and many perspectives of the organization (Bailey, Kaplan & Weinberg 2012; Laudon & Laudon 2005, p. 523). The explosive growth of the Internet use by businesses and individuals has been accompanied by rising concerns of security breach and identity theft. Corporate and personal information is at a higher risk of theft and misuse than ever before as a result of the global connectedness.

However organizations have not given sufficient attention to security issues. According to Carnegie Mellon 2012 CyLab's global survey on how boards and senior management are governing their organizations' information assets (digital assets) (cited in Westby 2012, p. 5), "57% of them are not analysing the adequacy of cyber insurance coverage or undertaking key activities related to cyber risk management to help them manage reputational and financial risks associated with the theft of confidential and proprietary data and security breaches". In addition, on top of potential legal implications (more and sophisticated regulations for protecting information and privacy are being established around the world), the reputational and financial losses arising from a breach could be significant. The results of the survey also showed that the majority of organizations still lag in establishing key positions for properly looking at privacy, risk and security risks (such as Chief Information Security Officer, Chief Security Officer, Chief Privacy Officer, and Chief Risk Offier). The 2011 U.S. Cost of a Data Breach Study by Symantec and the Ponemom Institute (cited in Westby 2012, p. 11) indicated that the data breach cost firms an average of US$ 5.5 million per incident, and another recent study by Ponemom Institute (cited in Westby 2012, p. 11) pointed out a data breach could cost organizations 17-30% loss of brand and reputation, and such damage to corporate image could take them more than a year to recover.

To deal with various security challenges arising from the use of information technology and protect our information resources, it requires a variety of security tools and defensive measures and a coordinated security management program, including hardware, software, policies, and procedures. Some security measures and tools adopted by organizations include: Biometrics (i.e., Vein ID, finger prints, Iris Scan, face recognition, speech recognition), password, swipe card & other tools for physical access control, Antivirus software/applications, Virtual private networks, Firewalls, Identity management and access control systems, Encryption, Tokenization & Key Management, Intrusion detection systems, Online access control, Information Security Plan, Network security protocols, Data backup, Data loss prevention systems (for monitoring data moving on the corporate network), Information security plan, Regular security plan testing, Security plan compliance audit, Information systems control & audit, Risk Management & Cyber Risk Insurance, Security & Privacy risks committees, C-level positions (i.e., Chief Information Officer, Chief Security/Information Security Officer, Chief Privacy Officer, Chief Risk Officer, Chief Trust Officer) (O'Brien & Marakas 2011, p. 534 & 538; Laudon & Laudon 2005; p. 542; Laseter & Johnson 2011; Westby 2012, Authors' own knowledge). Meanwhile, the larger the organisation and the more sensitive of the information (i.e., information in certain government intelligence gathering agencies), the increased risk and costs of security breaches, and thus more comprehensive, systematic, integrated and sophisticated security (and privacy) measures need to be put into place. Westby (2012, p. 26) provides some recommendations for governing enterprise security management:

- Establish a board Risk Committee for managing enterprise risks (including IT risks) and recruit directors with security, IT governance and cyber risk expertise.
- Ensure privacy and security roles are separated and their responsibilities are appropriately assigned.
- Establish a cross-organizational team and discuss privacy and security issues at least once every moth.

- Create a culture of security and respect for privacy and view security and privacy as a corporate social responsibility.
- Ensure the quality of security program by regularly reviews and taking into consideration of best practices and industry standards.
- Ensure the security and privacy requirements to third parties and vendors.
- Conduct annual audit of enterprise security program by relevant committees and act on identified gaps.
- Require regular security and privacy reports for board and senior executives.
- Assess cyber risks and potential loss valuations and Review adequacy of cyber insurance coverage.
- Allocate sufficient resources for security and privacy programs

Haag, Baltzan and Phillips (2008, pp. 330–339) suggest organisations can implement information security lines of defence through people first and technology second. They point out that most information security breaches result from people misusing an organisation's information either advertently or inadvertently. Their views are supported by Laseter and Johnson (2011), who believe the root causes of many security breaches are done by insiders. The first line of defence an organisation should follow is to create an information security plan detailing the various information security policies. Steps to creating an information security plan include (Haag, Baltzan & Phillips 2008, p. 333):

1. Developing the information security policies
2. Communicating the information security policies
3. Identifying critical information assets and risks
4. Testing and re-evaluating risks
5. Obtaining stakeholder support.

Information systems should be periodically examined, or audited, by a company's internal auditing staff or external auditors from professional accounting firms. Such audits should review and evaluate whether proper and adequate security measures and management policies have been developed and implemented (Laudon & Laudon 2005, p. 542).

Many of the detrimental effects of information technology are caused by individuals or businesses that are not accepting ethical responsibility for their actions. Managers, business professionals, and information systems specialists as well as end users must accept their ethical responsibilities and practice ethically. Protecting private information is an increasingly challenging and critical issue in today's networked economy. For example, a personal e-health record could include such information as: (1) demographic information (including your name, date of birth, vital statistics such as height, weight, blood pressure, and pulse rate), (2) a list of emergency contacts as well as contacts for all of your health care providers, (3) information about your health insurance, (4) a brief history of your health, along with a list of illness and conditions your parents, grandparents, and siblings ever had, (5) information about allergies or sensitivities to medications, (6) a dated list of significant illness and hospitalizations, (7) your current health conditions and how they are being treated, (8) an inventory of the medication you take, including dosages and frequency, (9) a dated list of immunizations, and (10) copies of your living will and durable power of attorney for health care, if you have them (Halamak 2009). According to one recent survey of Harris Poll (cited in Sadauskas 2012) looking at how comfortable consumers are with the way of Facebook, Amazon and Google are handling their personal data, 66% of survey participants were comfortable with Amazon's use of previous visits for recommendations while only 41% and 33% of respondents agree with Google's use of prior website visits for displaying advertisements and Facebook's use of private data for advertising purposes.

Ethics are 'the principles and standards that guide our behavior toward other people' (Haag, Baltzan & Phillips 2008, p. 344). O'Brien & Marakas (2011, p. 531) suggest that when making ethical decisions in business issues, managers can look at several important ethical dimensions, such as equity, rights, honesty and exercise of corporate power. Even though there are some information related laws, organisations often face the dilemma of being ethical versus being legal. This is complicated by the fact that information systems are emerging, changing and growing in such unexpected ways (Haag, Baltzan & Phillips 2008, p. 344). Laudon & Laudon (2005 p. 154) suggest some technology trends which raise ethical issues for information systems use. They are:

- Computing power doubles every month: organisations increasingly depend on computer systems for critical operations
- Rapidly declining data storage costs: organisations can easily maintain detailed information on individuals
- Data analysis advances: companies have the ability to analyse vast quantities of data gathered on individuals to develop detailed profiles of individual behaviour
- Networking advances and the Internet: it is much easier to copy data from one location to another and to access personal data from remote locations.

Organisations strive to build a corporate culture based on ethical principles that employees can understand and implement. Policies and procedures addressing the ethical issues of the use of information technology, including ethical computer use policy, information privacy policy, acceptable use policy, email privacy policy, Internet use policy, and anti-spam policy, should be established. Haag, Baltzan andPhillips (2008, p. 348) state 'These policies set employee expectations about the organization's practices and standards and protect the organization from misuse of computer systems and computing resources'. They also point out that 'Information has no ethics' (p. 346). Individuals form the only ethical component of an information system. How they use the system, how they are affected by the system and how their use of the system affects other people is largely determined by their ethics.

1.4.2 *Other critical information systems management issues*

On top of the above mentioned issues, some other critical information systems issues include:

- Digital Divide: Today more than 70% of the world's citizens live in the societies which are just in the beginning stage of digitization (Mainardi 2012). The Networked Readiness Index reflects the degree of to which economies leverage ICT for enhanced competitiveness and is measured by four dimensions of environment (political and regulatory environment, business and innovation environment), readiness (infrastructure and digital content, affordability, skills), usage (individual usage, business usage, and government usage), impact (economic impacts and social impacts) (Dutta, Bilbao-Osorio & Geiger 2012, pp. 3–7). Most of advanced economies (i.e., Sweden, Singapore, Finland, Denmark, Switzerland, Netherlands, Norway, United States, Canda, and United Kingdom are top 10 NRI countries) have high Networked Readiness Index, and many sub-saharan African countries have very low ICT readiness with main reason of insufficient development of ICT infrastructure, which still remains very costly. In addition, for Baby Boomers, Generation Y, Generation X, Generation C, So called "Digital Natives", 21st Centuriers, and beyond, what are their relations with IS/IT?. As Kleiner (2012) argues for digital generation (those under 25 and are always-on), digital channel is definitely preferred way of doing everything, and having to go offline is viewed as an annoyance.
- Internet Governance: Open access approaches and infrastructure sharing are likely to be the foundations for future network (Biggs *et al.* 2012, p. 51). Some countries (e.g., Australia, Malaysia, Qatar, Singapore) have embarked on creating entirely new national broadband networks (deploying fibre optic technology throughout the core network), and investments in those networks are huge (e.g., Australia's NBN will cost AU$ 43 billion).

Currently we are in a mixed mode policy environment where self-regulation, through a variety of Internet policy and technical bodies, co-exists with limited government regulation. As Eric Smith, Former CEO and now Chairman of Google argues (reported in Manyika 2008), there will not be easy to establish international agreement on Internet governance (for example, what is appropriate or legal in one country could be inappropriate and illegal in another country) since various legal and political challenges will be involved. It is not ture that the Internet cannot be controlled – in fact, the Internet can be very easily controlled, monitored, and regulated from a central location (such as done by China, Singapore, and others). Primary questions are: (1) who will control Internet and e-commerce and (2) what elements will be controlled and how. Internet Neutrality/Net Neutrality: Currently all Internet traffic treated equally (or neutrally)—all activities charged the same rate, no preferential assignment of bandwidth. However firms such as telcoms would like to be able to charge differentiated prices based on the amount of bandwidth consumed by the content-in other words, Internet usage should be charged as the usage of other utilities such as electricity, water, gas, especially for heavy users.

- Work-life balance: nowadays the line between leisure and work has become blurred. The technologies and the networks have made the work and the home life inseparable-for example, how often do you check your mobile phone? Your email accounts? Your social network pages? Surfing the net?
- Less-human: "Nobody knows you are a dog on the web" (have we become less human and more represented only by a series of the number of 0 and the number of 1?; have the technologies and the Internet made us stupid?; have we lost our ability of writing and thinking and over relied on computing devices and the Web?; how much do you believe statements/concept such as the Internet is a brain?; the network is a computer?; the Web is the Internet?; and the hybrid human or machine-the mix of human flesh and IS/IT?).
- Digital referencing and monitoring: One recent CareerBuilder survey (reported in Ferguson 2012) indicated that employers have been searching information on job applicants and interview candidates online and using such information for hiring decision. Survey respondents (from HR departments/functions) suggested they have used online information for not hiring a candidate, the reported such information for not hiring decision includes: 49% shared provocative or in appropriate photos or information, 45% listed information about drinking or using drugs, 35% had poor communication skills, 33% had mouthed a previous employer, and 28% made discriminatory comments. In addition, applications

(i.e., Digital Mirror) are now available for organizations to model people's digital communication style and monitor their digital behaviour at work (Ferguson 2012).

- Long Tail versus Power Law: as Eric Smith, Former CEO and now Chairman of Google argues (reported in Manyika 2008) while organizations need both tails (referring to long tail theory suggested by Chris Anderson in his book titled 'The Long Tail: why the Future of Business is Selling Less for More") and heads, the majority of revenue remains in the head (i.e., some core products and services for a business). He also suggests the Internet will likely follow the power law and lead to more concentration (i.e., a few major players and brands). His views are supported by Elberse (2008), who suggests organizations should focus on their most popular products and services since most of the revenue will come from them, and the niche products (in the long tail) should not be the focus unless the organization wants to satisfy the appetite of its heavy and frequent customers, who are interested in products and services in both the head and then the tail.

1.5 Emerging Trends and Future Directions

In the 21st century, organisations are facing more uncertainty than ever. Technological change is one of the primary sources of this uncertainty. Haag, Baltzan and Phillips (2008, p. 430) state that good understanding of emerging trends and new technologies can provide organizations with valuable strategic advantages. Those organizations that can most effectively grasp the deep currents of technological evolution are in the better position to protect them against sudden and fatal technological obsolescence. For them, technologies that will have the greatest impact on future business include digital ink, digital paper, teleliving, alternative energy sources, and autonomic computing, and trends that will have the greatest impact on future business include (Haag, Baltzan & Phillips 2008, pp. 431–435; 435–439):

- The world's population will double in the next 40 years' mostly in developing countries.
- The population in developed countries is living longer.
- Growth in information industries creates a knowledge-dependent global society.
- The global economy is becoming more integrated.
- The economy and society are dominated by technology.
- Pace of technological innovation is increasing.
- Time is becoming one of the most precious commodities.

1.5.1 *Ten working forces in 2020*

According to research into the workplace of the future, Fredette *et al.* (2012, pp. 116–117) suggest ten working forces in 2020:

- Demographics: there will be five generations working side by side
- The knowledge economy: except domain knowledge, a significant more complex set of interdisciplinary skills will be required.
- Globalization: by 2020, companies will rely on global marketplace rather than domestic or even international marketplace to fuel growth.
- The digital workplace: employees will find easier to create and access digital assets of the organization.
- Mobile technology: organizations could do more via mobile (smart) phones.
- Culture of connectivity: Hyper-connectivity will result in a connectivity culture in businesses and in our personal life.
- Participation: improved collaboration and knowledge/information sharing will foster a participating society.
- Social learning: Learning 3.0 (also called social learning), which incorporates social media, gaming, real-time feedback and simulation, would be used for teaching and learning purposes.
- Corporate social responsibilities: an increased cultural intelligence and a deeper appreciation of the relationship between business and society.
- The Millennial generation: This generation has grown up with hyper-connectivity and embracing it is an integral part of their life.

1.5.2 *Technology-enabled threats and trends*

According to a recent global survey of 864 executives from different industries and regions (reported in Roberts & Sikes 2011), some technology-enabled threats to organizations include (in the order):

- Rising customer expectations (for better or differentiated services)
- Significant changes in delivery costs (competitors' delivering for significantly less)
- Developing new offerings outside the business's traditional scope (i.e., mobile payment systems)
- Significantly improved products or services (including substitutes) from competitors with existing or lower prices

- Emergence of new channels or points of purchase
- Increased bargaining power for customers as a result of the easy access to the information
- Increased use of third-party computing resources/infrastructure

The survey results also indicate measures organizations have taken or plan to take in response to continuing economic uncertainty. Those measures include:

- Increasing infrastructure consolidation or virtualization
- Looking to information systems as a lever to reduce costs in other areas of the business
- Focusing on efficiency improvements in application development (i.e., lean approach and process streamlining)
- Renegotiating existing vendor contracts
- Increasing outsourcing and/or offshoring
- Reducing demand by cancelling or deferring projects/activities
- Rationalizing or eliminating services or/and reducing service levels
- Changing the scope of projects to reduce costs

Bughin, Chui and Manyika (2010) present ten technology-enabled business trends executives need to understand and respond to:

- Wide adoption of distributed co-creation: organizations need to effectively use online communities to develop, market, and support products and services.
- Making the network the organization: networked organizations need to have embrace open innovation and take full advantage of the opportunities of tapping into a world of talent" (accessing expertise within and outside the organization). They also need to break down silos in the organization and focus on the orchestration of the tasks rather than existing organizational structure and the ownership of workers.
- Deeper collaboration: organizations need to leverage the productivity of knowledge workers by having technologies such as video conferencing, shared workspaces, virtual teams, and virtual organizations.
- The growing Internet of Things: organizations need to utilizing the ability of capturing, computing, communicating, and collaborating information at large scale in real time provided by radio frequency identification tags, sensors and similar things embedded in the devices to improved capabilities of information collection & analysis and monitoring & responding.
- Using Big Data for experimenting and business intelligence: organizations need to effectively collect data from various sources (especially social data), analyse data, understand

the implications of the results of data analysis, and use such information for improving operations, and enhancing business performance.
- Paying close attention to Green and Sustainable information systems: organizations need to actively work on reducing carbon emission from computing facilities (i.e., by adopting virtualization technologies to reduce the number of servers, using natural air for the cooling of data centers, using renewable energy (such as hydroelectric power, wind and solar energy) for powering data centers, only using environmental friendly components to build computing devices) and using information systems for reducing environmental stress (i.e., via smart meters to better allocate energy usage, smart grids to improve the efficiency of transmission and distribution of energy, smart buildings to monitor and optimize energy uses, powerful analytic software to improve logistics and routing for planes, trains, trucks to reduce the carbon footprint of transportation.
- Wide adoption of the service model of Paying only for what you use (as per usage): organizations (large and small) could actively pursue cloud computing and outsourcing options as a result of the global connectedness and the available technologies for effectively organizing, monitoring, measuring, customizing and billing for computing assets.
- The age of multisided business model (generating revenue from giving something free): organizations need to leverage on the network effects and learn to create value (i.e., revenue or insights on customers via large volume information collected) from large traffic and large customer base developed from free services.
- Creating opportunities from the bottom of pyramid: organizations need to have the skills to identify and prosper from extreme market conditions (i.e., customer demand for low prices, poor infrastructure, hard-to-access suppliers and low cost curve for talent) by developing technology-enabled solutions (i.e., deploying mobile payment systems for African countries in which Internet access is a luxury for many people; developing B2B online platforms like Alibaba.com for buyers to source cheap products and services from low cost suppliers; virtual research and service teams by tapping into low cost talent in some developing countries).
- Using technology for government services and community support: technology-enabled solutions such as e-government, smart community, e-learning, e-health, e-police, smart water grids should be provided to the public, but it should be a joint effort of government agencies, communities, organizations and individuals.

They further suggest that only understanding and adopting these technology-enabled trends is not sufficient, organizations need to strategically work on their organizational culture and structure as well as management practices to meet these new demands. In addition, the significance and approach for fostering unfamiliar collaboration with non-traditional partners is should be clearly communicated to all the parties involved.

Brynjofsson and McAfee (2012) predict four emerging technologies having a large impact on the business in the coming decade:

- Inexpensive industry robots: better and more affordable robots will be used for industrial and life purposes.
- Voice recognition and translation software: full-ledged digital assistants translating for us while we travel will be a reality in the near future.
- Sophisticated automated response systems: computing devices will be smarter by learning from Big Data and in the future more machines will perform better than IBM's supercomputer Watson who beat human champions in the show of Jeopardy! In 2011.
- Autonomous vehicles: self-moving cars (more affordable and improved version of Google's expensive prototype of self-driving car) will be common phenomenon.

1.5.3 *Digital business*

We are in the digital economy in which digitization is an essential part of the way we live, work and conduct the business. In line with the potential opportunities and the rapid development of digitization, many organizations have set up designated position for their digitization efforts, such as Head of Strategy & Programs for Digital Innovation, Philips; EVP, Digital Strategy & Emerging Business, Discovery Communications; VP, Digital Banking Strategy, Wells Fargo; EVP, Digital Media, BET Networks; VP, Digital Strategy, BAE Systems; VP, Digital Marketing & Media, GSN; Director, Digital Marketing & Communication, PBS; VP, Innovation, Deutsche Telelkom; VP, Digital, Technology R & D, UFC; VP, Digital Strategy, Dell; CTO, Digital Operations, Education Week; VP, Audience Insights, TiVO; Director, Digital Strategy, Rodale Grow; Director, Online Strategy & Media, The Story Stuff Project; Global Head of Social Media, Bloomberg; among many others.

1.5.3.1 *The tangible contributions by the Internet*

According to one recent research conducted by consulting firm McKinsey (cited in Hazan, Manyika & Pelissie du Rausas 2011), from 2005 to 2009, the Internet is accounted for 21% of combined GDP growth of nine developed economies (including Sweden, Germany, United Kingdom, France, South Korea, United States, Italy, Canada, and Japan). Organizations need to actively look for opportunities unlocked by the Internet, such as reinventing business models to leverage the global connectedness, exploring emerging Internet-related trends and technologies (i.e., the Internet of Things) to improve the efficiency of business operations, and embracing new and flexible organizational structure via linking with employees, customers, suppliers and business partners (Hazan, Manyika & Pelissie du Rausas 2011).

1.5.3.2 Digital Transformation

The IBM 2010 Global CEO study (cited in Berman & Bell 2011, p. 1) identified that technology was second only to market factors as a force for change. According to IBM Institute for Business Value (cited in Berman & Bell 2011, p. 2), evolution of digital transformation has so far gone through three stages:

- Stage 1 (from late 1990s): digital products (i.e., music, entertainment) and infrastructure (i.e., telecommunications, software, information systems)
- Stage-2 (around 2000s): digital distribution and web strategy (i.e., e-commerce, online services)
- Stage-3 (around 2010s): mobile revolution, social media, hyper digitization, and power of analytics.

They also suggest nowadays people are using mobile devices and interactive tools to decide who to trust, where to go and what to buy. They have been increasingly empowered by the capability and convenience of accessing information anytime and anywhere, their expectations have risen dramatically, and they have now become the primary force behind digital transformation across industries.

1.5.3.3 Organization's readiness for digital transformation

How do you assess your organization's readiness for digital transformation. Berman and Bell (2011, p. 10) suggest the following questions from two perspectives of reshaping customer value proposition and optimizing operation to be looked at:

- How are you engaging with customers to understand their needs and expectations? And how they are changing in the digital environment?
- How will you drive the digital agenda in your industry rather than having it imposed on you by competitors?
- How do you integrate online and social media touch points, customer information and insights across your entire enterprise?

- What are you doing to make sure you are putting the customer at the center of your supply chain planning and execution every time?
- How are you realizing the benefits of open collaboration-within your enterprise, with customers and with partners?
- How are you optimizing your digital and physical (non-digital) components across all aspects of your operating model?

1.5.3.4 *Digital transformation capabilities*

IBM Institute for Business Value (cited in Berman & Bell 2011, p. 11) suggests six capabilities of digital transformation:

- Business model innovation: building customer value as a core competency.
- Customer and community collaboration: engaging with customers fully via various channels and touch points.
- Cross-channel integration: integrating digital and non-digital channels.
- Insights from analytics: taking advantage of the predicative power of Big Data and advanced analytics to the Big Data.
- Digitally enabled supply chain: optimizing and integrating all components of supply chain.
- Networked workforce: getting the right skills around the right business opportunities.

1.5.3.5 *Digitization and prosperity*

Reported in El-Darwiche, Singh & Genediwalla (2012), in 1990, there were 100 million PCs worldwide, 10 million mobile phone users, and less than 3 million Internet users; but by 2010 there were 1.4 billion personal computers, 5 billion mobile phone users, and 2 billion Internet users.

El-Darwiche, Singh and Genediwalla (2012) argue that the national economic growth is associated with the adoption of information and communications technology, and suggest countries that have achieved mass adoption of digital technologies and ICT applications by individuals, businesses, and governments (in other words, advanced level of digitization) have realized significant economic, social, and political benefits. They further point out that countries with most advanced digitization development which is measured by such factors as ubiquity (the level of access to digital services and applications), affordability (pricing), reliability (the quality of connection), speed (the rate of data throughput), usability (how easy is to get online and use online applications/services), and skills (the ability of users to incorporate digital applications and services into their lives and businesses), could derive 20% more in economic benefits than those who are in the beginning stage.

1.5.3.6 Digitization and its impact

According to Sabbagh *et al.* 2012 (p. 122), digitization can be measured across six key attributes:

- Ubiquity (the extent to which consumers and enterprises have universal access to digital services and applications): could be measured by fixed broadband penetration, mobile phone penetration, mobile broadband penetration, personal computers, population penetration, and 3G mobile connection penetration.
- Affordability (the extent to which digital services are priced in a range that makes them available to as many people as possible): could be measured by fixed line installation cost, fixed cost per minute, mobile connection fee, mobile prepaid tariff, and fixed broadband Internet access tariff.
- Reliability (the quality of available digital services): could be measured by investment per subscriber (mobile broadband and fixed line).
- Speed (the extent to which digital services can be accessed in real time): could be measured by international Internet bandwidth and broadband speeds
- Usability (the ease of use of digital services and the ability of local ecosystems to boost adoption of these services): could be measured by Internet retail as % of total retail, E-government web measure index, % of individuals using the Internet, Data as % of wireless ARPU (average revenue per user), domains by country per 100 inhabitants, IP addresses per 100 inhabitants, social network unique visitors per month, and average SMS usage per customer.
- Skills (the ability of users to incorporate digital services into their lives and businesses): could be measured by the number of engineers per 100 inhabitants, % of labour force with more than secondary education.

Meanwhile they (Sabbagh *et al.* 2012, p. 126) suggest the impact of digitization could be looked at from three perspectives:
- Economy (the impact of digitization on the growth of economy): measured by GDP growth, job creation, and innovation.
- Society (the impact of digitization on the society well-being of a country): measured by quality of life and access to basic services.

- Governance (the impact of digitization on public sector): measured by transparency of government operations and business activities, E-government, and education.

1.5.4 *Some other trends*

Meanwhile some other trends include:
- The Speed of Growth: In recent years, young tech start-ups can grow at a dizzying pace, for example firms like Groupon grow to a multiple billion firm within three years. Ron Conway (cited in Conway 2012), special advisor to SV Angel reckons that in 2012, we may see a firm developing into a US$ one billion business within 12 months.
- The Global Grid: Organizations need to think about opportunities arising from the global connectedness (of course associated impacts as well). On this global grid, every company is now a global company and have the potential to leverage the power of more than 4 billion connected minds (Bisson, Stephenson & Patrick Viguerie 2010).
- Machine versus Human intelligence: even though machines will be more self-aware through machine learning and other approaches and be smarter in the future while we keep on feeding them with Big Data and continuously improve algorithms and methodologies, human being will still be in charge of the world, as Eric Smith, Former CEO and now Chairman of Google argues (reported in Manyika 2008). The former will be good at high volume analytical and replication work while the latter will always be excel at works requiring intuition, experiences, and insights.
- SoLoMo (coined by John Doerr, Venture Capitalist and Partner of Kleiner Perkins Caufield & Byers, reported in Kleiner 2012): Social, Local and Mobile computing is the way to go; smart phones could connect and locate people as well recognizing whom they are connecting to and businesses could have more targeted advertisements as well, providing more personalized and customized products and services through social, local and mobile computing capabilities.
- Cloud Computing & Agile Development: Organizations are embarking on cloud computing and agile development as well as other flexible delivery approaches and platforms to better utilize their information systems investments; have better flexibility, quicker responses to changes, enhanced ability for information systems to scale up, better ability of disaster recovery and business continuity; and focus on their core business (especially for small and medium firms).
- Big Data and Analytics: Gathering and analysing large (or very large) volume data is quickly becoming popular organizations for reasons such as large volume data from

multiple channels and various sources, the need for better understanding customers, and the tangible benefits of gaining competitive advantages by doing this (i.e., the success of Amazon, Google) (Bughin, Livingston & Marwaha 2011).

- Content Business: In today's digital economy, almost every firm is in the business of content creation (Berman & Bell 2011).
- Social Computing/Social Commerce: According to one recent study by McKinsey Global Institute (reported in Chui *et al.* 2012, p. 142), one third of global consumer spending could be influenced by social media. According to IBM Institute for Business Value (cited in Berman & Bell 2011), 89% of millennial generation and 72% of baby boomers use social networking sites, and the gap is closing.
- Hyper-connectivity: Hyper-connectivoity has several key attributes (Fredette *et al.* 2012, p. 113): always on, readily accessible, information rich, interactive, not just about people (including the Internet of things), and always recording. According to Dutta, Bilbao-Osorio & Geiger (2012, p. 3) the exponential growth of mobile devices, Big Data, and social media are all drivers of hyper-connectivity.
- Human skills remained in demand: Even though computers are getting better, powerful and smarter, they are only good at certain things (i.e., pattern recognition, processing of large volume data, complex communications), they are still not good at many things requiring intuition, judgment, experience, and insight. Some examples include: applied math & statistics (computers can't decide what analyses to carry out and how to interpret the results), negotiation & group dynamics, good writing, framing problems &solving open-ended problems, persuasion, and human interaction & nurturing (Brynjofsson & McAfee 2012).
- Green information systems: Green information systems are also an emerging trend. Do you know 'performing two Google searches can generate a similar amount of carbon dioxide to boiling the kettle for a cup of tea'? (Leake & Woods 2009). According to IDC (cited in Trepant, Chow and Baker 2008), U.S. firms spend close to US$ 6 billion on the power needed to run data centers and another 3.5 billion to air-condition them. Trepant, Chow & Baker (2008) suggest organizations (such as Google notably) have used alternative sources of energy (i.e., wind, hydraulic) to power their data centres and have adopted technologies (such as virtualization) to better and more utilize servers to achieve savings in energy and reduce carbon emissions. They further argue organizations should adopt an EIP (environmental impact planning) system to monitor the environmental impacts of their business activities. Green information system (Eco-information systems) solution/approach not only

reduces the costs for the organization, but also shifts IT from a cost player to revenue player when more and more consumers are considering the environmental impact of the products they purchase. According to Babcock (2010, p. 10), it is estimated Google could have 500,000 to 600,000 servers across its 12 international data centers; and Microsoft is building a largest data center on earth with 300, 000 servers. He also suggests energy could make up 20% of the running cost of a data cener (p. xiii).

- Mobile Computing/Mobile Commerce/Location: El-Darwiche, Singh & Genediwalla (2012) suggest that more people today have access to a mobile phone than to electricity. With more than 6 billion connections worldwide and US$ 1.3 trillion in revenue, mobile telephony has become the largest ICT industry in history and surpassed the landline Internet by more than 3.5 billion users (Dutta & Bilbao-Osorio 2012). One significant element of mobile commerce is mobile payment systems (i.e., Google's Google Wallet, Amazon's Amazon Checkout, Paypal's mobile payment systems). For factors such as the wide adoption of mobile phones and devices (especially iPads), technologies such as NFC (near field communication), QR Codes, GPS applications, Augment reality (i.e., Google Goggles, Layar, and Wikitude), the popularity of mobile applications (i.e., i-tunes and games), and the convenience of paying anytime and anywhere without waiting in the checkout line, mobile payments have become an essential part of today's networked economy. Currently there are more than 500 million mobile phone subscribers in Africa (Mainardi 2012). According to ABI Research (reported in Van Dyk 2012), while comparing with developed economies it has much fewer banks and ever fewer ATMS, Africa is a leader in mobile commerce. Mobile banking and mobile transactions is a standard there. Kenya only started its mobile commerce program in 2007, but 20% of country's GDP are transacted via simple text messages from mobile phones. Meanwhile tablet-computers are getting popular among individual and business users. According to JP Morgan (cited in The Economist 2012), driven by the popularity of iPads, the table-computer market will reach US$ 35 billion in 2012 (from virtually nothing in 2009).

1.6 Summary

In this Chapter, we examined some important concepts of information systems. The key distinctions between information resources and traditional tangible resources were discussed. The required information systems competence for managers was explored as well. With the increasing role of information systems in business, government, and daily life, organisations have to address critical issues of information systems (i.e., security and privacy concerns) when they develop and implement their information system solutions. Information systems can be a double-edged sword. While it can bring us many benefits (especially the Internet-enabled capabilities), it also create new opportunities for unethical and immoral behaviours. Organisations have to take steps to protect the accuracy, reliability, security and accessibility of their information resources. Finally, we looked at emerging technologies and future directions of IS/IT, which are important for the organization's sustainable growth in the 21st century. In the next chapter, we will discuss how information systems can help organisations gain competitive advantages.

Bibliography

Babcock, C. 2010, *Management Strategies for the Cloud Revolution: How Could Computing Is Transforming Business and Why You Can't Afford to Be Left Behind*, McGraw-Hill, USA.

Bailey, T., Kaplan, J. & Weinberg, A. 2012, 'Playing war games to prepare for a cyberattack', *McKinsey Quarterly*, July 2012, pp. 1–6.

Berman, SJ & Bell, R 2011, 'Digital Transformation: Creating New Business Models Where Digital Meets Physical', *IBM Global Business Service Executive Report*, IBM Institute for Business Value, pp. 1–17.

Biggs, p. , Johnson, T., Lozanova, Y. & Sundberg, N. 2012, 'Emerging issues for our hyperconnected world', in *The Global Information Technology Report 2012: Living in a Hyper-connected World*, Dutta, S. & Bilbao-Osorio, B. eds., INSEAD & World Economic Forum, pp. 47–56.

Bisson, p. , Stephenson, E. & Patrick Viguerie, S. 2010, 'The global grid', *McKinsey Quarterly*, June 2010, pp. 1–7.

Bold, W. & Davidson, W. 2012, 'Mobile Broadband: Redefining Internet access and empowering individuals', in *The Global Information Technology Report 2012: Living in a Hyper-connected World*, Dutta, S. & Bilbao-Osorio, B. eds., INSEAD & World Economic Forum, pp. 67–77.

Brown, B. & Sikes, J. 2012, 'Minding your digital business', *McKinsey Global Survey Results*, McKinsey & Company 2012, pp. 1–9.

Brynjofsson, E. & McAfee, A. 2012, 'Winning the race with ever-smarter machines', *MIT Sloan Management Review*, Vol. 53, No. 2, pp. 53–60.

Bughin, J. Chui, M. & Manyika, J. 2010, 'Ten tech-enabled business trends executives need to watch to succeed', *McKinsey on Business Technology*, Number 20, Summer 2010, pp. 4–17.

Chui, M., Manyika, J., Bughin, J., Dobbs, R., Roxburgh, C., Sarrazin, H., Sands G. & Westergren, M. 2012, *The Social Economy: Unlocking Value and Productivity through Social Technologies*, McKinsey Global Institute, July 2012, pp. 1–170.

Conway, R. 2012, 'Where angels will tread', The World in 2012, *The Economist*, January 2012, p. 123.

Dutta, S. & Bilbao-Osorio, B. 2012, 'Executive Summary', in *The Global Information Technology Report 2012: Living in a Hyper-connected World*, Dutta, S. & Bilbao-Osorio, B. eds, INSEAD & World Economic Forum, pp. xi–xix.

Dutta, S., Bilbao-Osorio, B. & Geiger, T. 2012, 'The networked readiness index 2012: Benchmarking ICT progress and impacts for the next decade', in *The Global Information Technology Report 2012: Living in a Hyper-connected World*, Dutta, S. & Bilbao-Osorio, B. eds, INSEAD & World Economic Forum, pp. 3–34.

Eaton, J.J. & Bawden, D. 1991, 'What Kind of Resource Is Information', *International Journal of Information Management*, Vol. 11, No. 2, pp. 156–165.

Economist Intelligence Unit 2005, Business 2010: Embracing the Challenge of Change, Economist Intelligence Unit Ltd, February 2005, pp. 32.

El-Darwiche, B., Singh, M. & Genediwalla, S. 2012, 'Digitization and Prosperity', *Strategy + Business*, Issue 68, Autumn 2012, pp. 1–10.

Elberse, A. 2008, 'Should you invest in the long tail', *Harvard Business Review*, July-August 2008, pp. 88-96.

Enterprise Management Associates 2012, *The Industrialization of Fraud Demands a Dynamic Intelligence-Driven Response*, Enterprise Management Associates White Paper, March 2012, pp. 1–12.

Ferguson, R. B. 2012, 'The digital you at work: what to consider", *MIT Sloan Management Review*, 09/09/2012, Online Available at: http://sloanreview.mit.edu/improvisations/2012/09/09/the-digital-you-at-work-what-to-consider/ (accessed Sep 21, 2012).

Fredette, J., Marom, R., Setinert, K. & Witters, L. 2012, 'The promise and peril of hyperconnectivity for organizations and societies', in *The Global Information Technology Report 2012: Living in a Hyper-connected World*, Dutta, S. & Bilbao-Osorio, B. eds, INSEAD & World Economic Forum, pp. 113–119.

Haag, S., Baltzan, p. & Phillips, A. 2008, *Business Driven Technology*, 2nd edn, McGraw-Hill Irwin, Boston, USA.

Halamak, J. D. 'Your medical information in the digital age', *Harvard Business Review*, July-August 2009, pp. 22–23.

Hazan, E., Manyika, J. & Pelissie du Rausas, M. 2011, 'Sizing the Internet's economic impact', *McKinsey on Business Technology*, Number 24, Autumn 2011, pp. 18–21.

Kleiner, A. 2012, 'Brand transformation on the Internet', *Strategy + Business*, June 25, 2012, Online Available at: http://www.strategy-business.com/article/00117?pg=all (accessed July 20, 2012).

Kleiner, A. 2012, 'The thought leader interview: Bob Carrigan (CEO IDG Communications)', *Strategy + Business*, Issue 66, Spring 2012, pp. 1–8.

Laseter, T. & Johnson, E. 2011, 'A better way to battle Malware', *Strategy + Business*, Issue 65, Winter 2011, pp. 1–6.

Laudon, K.C. & Laudon, J.P. 2005, *Essentials of Management Information Systems: Managing the Dgital Firm*, 6th edn, Prentice Hall.

Laudon, K.C. & Laudon, J.P. 2012, *Management Information Systems: Managing the Digital Firm*, 12th edn, Prentice Hall.

Luftman, J. & Ben-Zvi, T. 2011, 'Key Issues for IT Executives 2011: Cautions Optimism in Uncertain Economic Times', *MIS Quarterly Executive*, Vol. 10, No. 4, pp. 203–212.

Mainardi, C. 2012, 'Forward', in *The Global Information Technology Report 2012: Living in a Hyper-connected World*, Dutta, S. & Bilbao-Osorio, B. eds, INSEAD & World Economic Forum, p. vii.

Manyika, J. 2008, 'Google's views on the future of business: An Interview with CEO Eric Schmidt', *McKinsey Quarterly*, September 2008, Online available at: https://www.mckinseyquarterly.com/Googles_view_on_the_future_of_business_An_interview_with_CEO_Eric_Schmidt_2229 (accessed Aug 2, 2012).

O'Brien, J. A. & Marakas, G. M. 2011, *Management Information Systems*, 10th Edition, McGraw-Hill, New York, USA.

Pearlson, K.E. & Saunders, C.S. 2004, *Managing and Using Information Systems: A Strategic Approach*, 2nd edn, Wiley, Danvers.

Ramakrishna, H.V., Vijayaraman, B.S. & Quarstein, V.A. 1995, 'Executives Speak out on MBA's Competency in Information Technology', *Journal of Systems Development*, Vol. 46, No. 2, pp. 14–17.

Roberts, R. & Sikes, J. 2011, 'How IT is managing new demands: McKinsey Global Survey results', McKinsey on Business Technology, Number 22, Spring 2011, pp. 24–33.

Sabbagh, K., Friedrich, R., El-Darwiche, B., Singh, M. & Ganediwalla, S. & Katz, R. 2012, 'Maximizing the impact of digitization', in *The Global Information Technology Report 2012: Living in a Hyper-connected World*, Dutta, S. & Bilbao-Osorio, B. eds., INSEAD & World Economic Forum, pp. 121–133.

Sadauskas, A. 2012, 'No faith in Facebook: US consumer confidence in social network plummets', *Smartompamy.com.au*, July 26, 2012, Online Available at: `http://www.smartcompany.com.au/information-technology/050900-no-faith-in-facebook-us-consumer-confidence-in-facebook-plummets.html` (accessed July 26, 2012).

Silver, M.S., Markus, M.L. & Beath, C.M. 1995, 'The Information Technology Interaction Model: A Foundation for the MBA Core Course', MIS Quarterly, September 1995, pp. 361–390.

The Economist (2012), 'The world in figures: industries', The World in 2012, *The Economist*, January 2012, pp. 117–118.

Trepant, H., Chow, G. & Baker, E. H. 2008, 'The Eco IT Solution', *Strategy + Business*, Issue 53, Winter 2008, pp. 1–3.

Turban, E, Lee, J.K., King, D., Liang, T.P. & Turban, D 2010, *Electronic Commerce: A Managerial Perspective 2010*, International edn, Prentice Hall, Upper Saddle River, USA.

Turban, E., King, D., Lee, J. Liang, T.P. & Turban, D. 2012, *Electronic Commerce: A Managerial and Social Networks Perspective 2012*, International edn, Prentice Hall, Upper Saddle River, NJ, USA.

Van Dyk, D. 2012, 'The end of Cash', *Time*, Vol. 179, No. 1, pp. 34–35.

Westby, J. R. (2012), 'How boards & senior executives are managing cyber risks', *Governance of Enterprise Security: CyLab 2012 Report*, Carnegie Mellon University CyLab, pp. 1–28.

Chapter 2
Information Systems for Competitive Advantages

This chapter will review competitive forces and competitive information systems strategies for gaining competitive advantages, explain concepts of value chain, value web and business ecosystems & co-opetition, and discuss innovation strategy.

2.1 Competitive Strategies

Gaining competitive advantage is critical for organisations. Baltzan and Phillips (2010, p. 16) define competitive advantage as 'a product or service that an organization's customers value more highly than similar offerings from its competitors' (in other words, you have something useful (i.e. products, services, capabilities) that your competitors do not have). Competitive advantages are typically temporary as competitors often seek ways to duplicate the competitive advantage (Baltzan & Phillips 2010, p. 16). In order to stay ahead of competition, organisations have to continually develop new competitive advantages. This section discusses how an organisation can analyse, identify, and develop competitive advantages using tools such as Porter's Five Forces, three generic strategies, and value chains.

Michael Porter's Five Forces Model is a useful tool to assist in assessing the competition in an industry and determining the relative attractiveness of that industry. Porter states that in order to do an industry analysis a firm must analyse five competitive forces (Baltzan & Phillips 2010, p. 17):

- Rivalry of competitors within its industry
- Threat of new entrants into an industry and its markets
- Threat posed by substitute products which might capture market share
- Bargaining power of customers
- Bargaining power of suppliers.

To survive and succeed, a business must develop and implement strategies to effectively counter the above five competitive forces. O'Brien and Marakas (2011, p. 49) suggest that organisations can follow one of five basic competitive strategies, which are based on Porter's three generic strategies of broad cost leadership, broad differentiation, and focused strategy. The five competitive strategies are: cost leadership, differentiation, innovation, growth, and alliance. Meanwhile, information systems could be a critical enabler of these five competitive strategies (see Table 2.1).

Table 2.1: Competitive Strategies & Roles of Information Systems

Competitive Strategy	Roles of Information Systems
Cost Leadership	Organizations can use information systems to fundamentally shift the cost of doing business (Booth, Roberts & Sikes 2011) or reduce the costs of business processes or/and to lower the costs of customers or suppliers, i.e., using online business to consumer & business to business models, e-procurement systems to reduce operating costs.
Differentiation	Organizations can use information systems to develop differentiated features or/and to reduce competitors' differentiation advantages, i.e., using online live chatting systems and social networks to better understand and serve customers; using technology to create informediaries to offer value-added service and improve customers' stickiness to your web site/business(Booth, Roberts, and Sikes 2011); applying advanced and established measures for online operations to offline practices (i.e., more accurate and systematic ways of measuring efficiency and effectiveness of advertising) (Manyika 2009).
	Continued on next page

Table 2.1 – continued from previous page

Competitive Strategy	Roles of Information Systems
Innovation	Organizations can use information systems to identify and create (or assist in creating) new products and services or/and to develop new/niche markets or/and to radically change business processes via automation (i.e., using digital modelling and simulation of product design to reduce the time and cost to the market (Chui & Fleming 2011). They also can work on new initiatives of establishing pure online businesses/operations. At the same time, the Internet and telecommunications networks provide better capabilities and opportunities for innovation. "Combinational innovation" and Open innovation are two good examples. There are a large number of component parts on the networks that are very expensive or extremely different before the establishment of the networks, and organizations could combine or recombine components/parts on the networks to create new innovations (Manyika 2009). Meanwhile everyone is connected via personal computers, laptops and other mobile devices through cabled Internet or wireless networks or mobile networks, there are plenty of opportunities to co-create with customers, external partners and internal people.
Growth (including mergers and acquisitions)	Organizations can use information systems to expand domestic and international operations or/and to diversify and integrate into other products and services, i.e., establishing global intranet and global operation platform; establishing omni-channel strategy to gain growth(omni-channel strategy looks at leveraging advantages of both online (or digital) and offline (or non-digital) channels) (Rigby 2011).
Strategic Alliance	Organizations can use information systems to create and enhance relations with partners via applications, such as developing virtual organizations and inter-organizational information systems.

(Source: Developed from O'Brien and Marakas 2011, pp. 49–51; Manyika 2009; Chui and Fleming 2011; Rigby 2011; Booth, Roberts, and Sikes 2011; The Authors' Own Knowledge)

On top of these five basic strategies, companies can also adopt other competitive strategies facilitated by information systems to shape their competitive advantage. Some examples include (O'Brien & Marakas 2011, p. 50–52; Chui & Fleming 2011; The Authors' Own Knowledge) are:

- Locking in customers or suppliers by enhancing relations and building valuable new relationships via customer/partner relationship management systems/ applications (i.e., providing a bank's customers with multiple touch points via telephones, Internet, fax machines, videos, mobile devices, ATMs, branches, the bank's agents).
- Building switching costs via extranets and proprietary software applications (i.e., Amazon's user-friendly and useful B2C website and Alibaba's B2B platform) so that a firm's customers or suppliers are reluctant to pay the costs in time, money, effort, and bear the inconvenience of switching to a company's competitors.
- Raising barriers to entry through improving operations or/and optimizing/flattening organizational structure by increasing the amount or the complexity of the technology required (i.e., Google's search engine and P & G's digitization strategy/efforts-P & G is working on digitizing almost every aspect of its operation to make it the world's most technologically enabled firm).

2.2 Value chain

Another important concept and tool that can help a business identify competitive advantage and opportunities for strategic use of information systems is Porter's value chain model. The value chain approach views an organisation as a chain, or series, of processes, and it classified an organization's activities into two categories: primary activities (i.e., inbound logistics, operations, sales & marketing, customer service, outbound logistics) and secondary/support activities (i.e., administration, human resources, technology, procurement) (O'Brien & Marakas 2011, p. 56; Laudon & Laudon 2012, p. 135). The value chain helps an organisation determine the 'value' of its business processes for its customers. The model highlights specific activities in the business where competitive strategies can be best applied and where information systems are most likely to have a strategic impact. By creating/adding value and thus creating competitive advantages, information systems could contribute to each part of an organization's value chain and extended value chain (including interactions/ties with external partners and strategic alliances). By leveraging on the Internet technologies, organizations could also create a value web (Laudon & Laudon

2012, p. 137) or a hub structure, both of them look at improving the efficiency and the effectiveness of value chain and supply chain by digitally connecting customers, suppliers, partners; by reducing the information gaps/errors along the chain (especially demand and supply); and by bettering communication, cooperation and collaboration.

2.3 Business Eco-systems and Co-opetition (Competition & Cooperation)

In today's digital era, firms need to have a more dynamic view of the boundaries among firms, customers, and suppliers, with both competition and cooperation occurring with members of the industry set (more than one industry) (Laudon & Laudon 2012, p. 140). For example, car, plane, bus, train are in the same industry set of transportation. Another example is the way that traditional universities are now competing with online learning and other training and development firms.

Business eco-systems refer to "loosely coupled but independent network of suppliers, distributors, partners and strategic alliances (Laudon & Laudon 2012, p. 139). An excellent example of business eco-systems is the mobile Internet platform; industries such as mobile device manufacturers, software vendors, online services firms, Internet services providers are working together. Meanwhile in order to stay ahead of the competition, organizations need to actively establish their business ecosystems. For example, looking at the competition between Apple and Sumsung, it can be said that Samsung is still very much a hardware player while Apple has been developing its ecosystem and venturing into areas of hardware, software, service, content and customer support in recent years (Wagstaff 2012). So who is doing better now?

Another term reflects the same meaning is "Co-opetition". In order to succeed in today's highly competitive market, firms also should practice 'co-opetition' since not all strategic alliances are formed with suppliers or customers. Co-opetition is a strategy whereby companies cooperate and compete at the same time with their competitors, complementors (i.e. hardware and software businesses), customers, suppliers (Pearlson & Saunders 2004, p. 52). Through co-opetition, the best possible outcome for a business can be achieved by optimally combining competition and cooperation. A good example is Co-visint (http://www.covisint.com/), which is the auto industry's e-marketplace and is backed up by competitors of GM, Ford, Daimler Chryslers and others. Benefits of Covisint include speed in decision-making, reduced supply chain costs and greater responsiveness in serving customers.

The downside to co-opetition is that it may be viewed as collusion. Many countries have legislation in force to deter anti-competitive or price-fixing practices. The Australian Competition & Consumer Commission (ACCC) in Australia has imposed huge monetary fines on companies and the directors of those companies found guilty of anti-competitive or price-fixing practices.

2.4 Innovation Strategy

2.4.1 *Open innovation strategy*

Open innovation emphasizes an organization's efforts of engaging and collaborating with external sources and its partners in its innovation process (Lichtenthaler, Hoegl & Muethel 2011). The telecommunications networks and Internet technologies have made the open innovation more appealing to organizations. Open innovation strategy has been adopted by many most innovative companies in the world. For example, 3M has been very successful in developing smart products via its open innovation approach- 10,000 R &D people in 73 locations from 63 full-scale operating businesses across dozens of industries work together as well as working with large number of external partners via 300 joint programs and customers via 30 customer technology centers around the world (Jaruzelski, Holman & Baker 2011).

One of the biggest barriers to promote open innovation in the organization is to do with employees' attitudes of not-invented here and not-sold-here, some strategies to deal with such attitudinal tendencies include (Lichtenthaler, Hoegl & Muethel 2011):

- Clearly communicating open innovation strategy across the organization, especially the benefits of opening up the innovation process to outside expertise.
- Demonstrated top management support: senior executives have to be champions and role models of open innovation strategy and simply providing lip services is not going to work.
- Establishing incentive/reward systems: need to reduce the traditional emphasis on internal-only innovation process and develop both monetary and non-monetary reward mechanism (i.e., granting open innovation award, providing opportunities to work in the partner organization for some time (especially in a different location/country) for open innovation practice.
- Fostering pro-open innovation environment by working on organizational culture and structure.

One of the excellent/prominent examples or leaders of successfully implementing open innovation strategy is Mozilla Corporation, which has developed an open-source and free web browser: Firefox (currently at its 14.0.1 version and accounts for more than 24% of web browsers market) (Wikipedia 2012). It has extensively relied on external people (a broader group of volunteers) outside the firm for creative ideas, development of products, and decision making (in fact the number of outside contributors is much larger than that of internal people). What are some recipes for Mozilla's huge success of open innovation strategy? Michelle Baker, Chairperson and former CEO of Mozilla Corporation provide with some answers (reported in Mendonca & Sutton 2008):

- Effectively managing the mode of participation: setting up frameworks where people can get involved in a very relaxed/decentralised way; having discipline in certain areas (i.e., programming codes going into the Firefox); putting quality control process in place; clearly specifying where input is needed; giving people the feeling of ownership thus inspiring their desire for creating an open, participatory and safe Internet.
- Balancing internal people and outside volunteers: you need both groups. Without the former Firefox won't be an established force while without the latter the Firefox project won't last for long.
- Having transparent and distributed decision-making process: decision-making process is unrelated to employment status (non-employees can also take part in the decision-making process).
- Having the confidence that giving people control or voice in an elegant manner can create innovations and generate good opportunities (even revenue).
- Open management style: giving up some control and turning people loose (of course you need to figure out appropriate space and range) could bring in great results beyond expectation. Leaders of the organization also need to have the courage to acknowledge they are not perfect and admit when they are wrong!

At the same time, by drawing on the experiences of successful open-source innovation initiatives (i.e., Wikipedia, ATLAS particle detector, Firefox web browser, Sun Microsystems' Solaris operating systems, and others), Bughin, Chui & Johnson (2008) present suggestions for effective open innovation management:

- Attracting and motivating co-creators/contributors: organizations need to effectively understand motivations of contributors and provide the right incentives to the right people. Participants are largely interested in making a contribution and seeing it become a reality. And many contributors do enjoy non-financial rewards, such as fun, fame/recognition, and

altruism. Trust and brand affinity are also important influencing factors. People generally don't want to work with brands/firms they don't trust or like.
- Appropriate structure for participation: projects/problems need to be broken down into smaller ones and let contributors work parallel on different pieces.
- Having governance mechanism to facilitate co-creation: clear rules, leadership, and transparent processes for setting goals and resolving conflicts should be established and clearly communicated.
- Quality assurance: a quality assurance process should be put into place.

In addition, managing risks of open innovation is another critical issue. One typical risk is intellectual property (IP). Organizations need to clearly understand potential IP risks and the investments/costs associated with identified risks, and could take measures such as establishing IP sharing agreement or/and rewards/risks sharing arrangement to deal with IP issues (Alexy & Reitzig 2012; Bughin, Chui & Johnson 2008). Updating & maintaining open source code and providing technical support to users are also needed to be looked at (Pearlson & Saunders 2010, p. 340).

2.4.1.1 *Google's way of innovation management*

Google is one of leaders in innovation management. What are some of its best practices? Google's Executive Chairman and former CEO Eric Schmidt provides us with some insights (reported in Manyika 2008):
- Believing the notion of wisdom of crowds argument: groups make better decisions than individuals, especially when the group are selected to be among the smartest and most interesting people.
- Having different views and always questioning/challenging established ways of doing thing: how can we do in different and better ways?
- Imposing a deadline: a good combination of flexibility and discipline is required, and both of them are essential.
- Perfecting the art of encouragement: we believe "the best ideas don't come from executives".
- Providing people with time for new ideas: we allocate 20% time for people to pursue their ideas.
- Having small and undirected teams for innovation and give people space and time for thinking and reflection: we believe "innovation always has been driven by a person or a

small team that has the luxury of thinking of a new idea and pursuing it... Innovation is something that comes when you are not under the gun...."

2.4.1.2 *Amazon's way of innovation management*

Amazon, which developed the innovated and most successful B2C e-commerce model, is another great example of innovation management. Some things organizations can learn from Amazon regarding innovation management include (Dumont, Kaura & Subramanian 2012: The Authors' Own Knowledge):

- Having business systems (can be easily broken into simpler sub-systems) and architecture (could be organized by simply plugging in modules and components) designed for rapid product development and quick responding to changes: Amazon has been successful in venturing into different areas and dealing with huge number of customers without diminishing service quality
- Having customer-centric mind-set: Amazon and its Zappos.com are examples of customer centric business-they provide what customers want and even beyond that...
- Having a good balance between control & speed and between vertical & horizontal integration to achieve differentiation and accelerate product cycles as well as venturing into new areas (especially adjacent markets).

2.4.1.3 *Apple's way of innovation management*

It could be argued that Apple's way of innovation management centres on two perspectives:

- Steve Job's innovation leadership
- User experience innovation developed through innovative product designs

2.4.2 **When does it make sense to be an early IS/IT adopter?**

Another important and highly debated topic in innovation strategy management is when organizations should be early adopter of new technologies. Companies like eBay (online auction), Yahoo (Internet directory), and Apple computer (software/hardware) 'got there first' and leveraged their first-mover/early adopter competitive advantage. Companies such as Citibank (ATM), Sony (video tape), Chemdex (B2B digital exchange), Netscape (Internet browser), lost their first-mover advantages to late movers. Intel (microchip), America Online (Internet marketing), and Google (online search engine) are some good examples of companies who were later movers but gained success over earlier adopters by being the best (Turban *et al.* 2006, p. 592).

The first mover in an industry has the advantage of being the first to offer a product or service to the market. This can help create an impression that the firm is the pioneer or the initiator in the customer's mind. In addition this firm will be able to capitalise on the demand for the product or service until another firm enters the market (Turban *et al.* 2006, p. 591). However, first movers take the risk that new goods and services may not be accepted by the market. Some suggested factors that determine the success or failure of the first mover strategy include (Turban *et al.* 2006, p. 591):

- Size of the opportunity: big enough opportunity for just one firm and the company is big enough for the opportunity
- Commodity products: simple enough to offer but hard to differentiate, i.e. books and airline seats. Products such as clothes and restaurants are more easily differentiated by later movers with better features and services encouraging a switch to late movers.
- Be the best: in the long run, best-mover advantage not first-mover advantage determines the market leader, such as Apple's iPhone, Google's search engine, Amazon's e-commerce platform.

In the long term, organisations have to keep on being innovative and investing in research and development (R & D) to stay ahead of the competition or even survive in the market. In fact, firms who are very active in innovation and seriously invest into their R &D are top performers. Some top spenders on R & D include: Toyota, General Motors, Ford, Honda, Volkswagan in the Auto industry; Pfizer, Johnson & Johnson, Roche Holding, GlaxoSmithKline, Novartis, Sanofi-Aventis, AstraZeneca, Merck in the Health Care industry; Nokia, Samsung, IBM, Intel, Panasonic, Cisco Systemsin the Computing and Electronics industry; Microsoft in the Software and Internet industry, and Siemens in the Industrials sector (Jaruzelski & Dehoff 2008; 2010; 2011; Jaruzelski, Loehr & Holman 2012). On the other hand, it is argued the success in innovation isn't really about how much money you spend but about how you spend (you need to spend wisely so you do better with less). For example the most innovative firms identified in the 2010 & 2011 Global Innovation 1000 study (reported in Jaruzelski & Dehoff 2011 and Jaruzelski, Loehr & Holman 2012 respectively) (such as in 2010 Apple (invested US$ 1,782 million/ 2.7% sales revenue into R & D activities), Google (3,762 million/12.8%), 3M (1,434 million/5.4%), and GE (3,939 million/2.6%); and in 2011 Apple (US$ 2.4 billion/2.2%), Google (5.2 billion/13.6%), 3M (1.6 billion/5.3%), Samsung (9.0 billion/6.0%) are serious about investing into R & D but they are not top spenders on R & D (such as in 2010 Roche Holding (9,466 million/21.1%), Pfizer (9,413 million/13.9%), Novartis (9,070 million/17.9%), Microsoft (8,714 million/14.0%; in 2011 Toyota (9.9 billion/4.2%), Novartis (9.6 billion/16.4%), Roche Holding (9.4 billion/19.6%), Pfizer (9.1 billion/13.5%)). Other factors influencing the success of innovation management include (Jaruzelski & Dehoff 2010; 2011; Jaruzelski, Loehr & Holman 2012): top management's innovation skills and attitude, innovation process (including effective management of ideas generation and the process of from idea generation to product development), alignment between innovation strategy and business strategy, and pro-innovation culture (i.e., strong customer focus and customer experience orientation, passion and pride for products and services offered). Among these five factors, top management's innovation skills and attitude is the most important one. If top leaders are not willing to and not good at innovation, then the chance of the success of organizational innovation efforts will be very slim, and they will not take the lead or do a good in developing innovation culture, establishing innovation process, and pushing the alignment between innovation strategy and business strategy.

While established brands do help organizations in the marketplace, it is the continuous innovation efforts have provided them with sustainable growth and competitive advantage. It is particularly true in some industries (such as media and publishing- many examples of failed traditional news and referencing materials publishers as a result of emerging digital content providers (i.e., Wikipedia, Google, Youtube and many others online players). Meanwhile when we are talking about innovation, we are referring not only to R & D for new products but also to changes and new things in the various parts of the business, such as business processes, customer services, marketing & sales, training & learning, talent management, knowledge management, data collection & decision-making, design of organizational structure, intra-organizational & inter-organizational communications, procurement, payment systems, logistics management, among many others.

Furthermore organizational learning (especially open learning) could be viewed as an important element of innovation, without effective and continuous learning and quick responses to market changes, organizations won't be able to have the skills and knowledge for creative ideas. It can be said that even though the success and failure of the business is a result of multiple factors including management issues (such as leadership, management experiences and skills, decision making process, investment strategies), organizational factors (such as culture, structure, processes, people's skills), changes in the industry and in the marketplace, and economic conditions, the ability and commitment to continuous innovation are definitely critical to the sustainable competitive advantage and long-term growth of the organization.

In fact, innovation is the source of the added-values and profits, for example Chinese manufacturers working on OEM orders typically make very slim margin while the owner of the intellectual property owner does much better. If an organization is able to make its innovation accepted as industry standard, then competitive advantages and good financial outcomes will be flowing in easily-just looking at the competition between Google's Android operation system and Apple's iOS (iphone operating system) for mobile devices.

Furthermore when we are talking about using IS/IT for innovation, IS/IT alone won't be enough for successful innovation, and it is a joint effort of IS/IT and business (users), which needs a top-down push to deal with silo problems and foster cooperation (Roberts & Sikes 2011). On a related note, Kleiner (2012) argues that only a few firms (i.e., Amazon, Apple) have successfully locked down their intellectual capital (technological information), and most companies hope that the speed of innovation beats the risk of leaking information to competitors. Continuous innovation could be used for dealing with intellectual property issues.

2.5 Summary

In this chapter an important dimension of information systems, identifying competitive advantages and enhancing competitive strategies through information systems, was discussed. Organisations can apply tools such as Porter's five forces and value chain to analyse their competitive position, examine their competitive advantages, and identify relevant competitive strategies. Information systems can play a very important role in the success of organisation's competitive strategies. However competitive strategies alone cannot create magic. In order to meet the 'IS/IT's unmet potential', both IS/IT and non-IS/IT executive need to work hard to have better understanding each other's areas (Roberts & Sikes 2008). The transparency in the planning and execution of information systems projects should be visible to business leaders. Accountability of information systems projects should be applied to both information systems and business parts in the organisation. In the next chapter, planning and evaluating information systems will be discussed.

Bibliography

Alexy, O. & Reitzig, M. 2012, 'Managing the business risks of open innovation', *McKinsey Quarterly*, January 2012, pp. 1–5.

Baltzan, p. & Phillips, A. 2010, *Business Driven Technology*, 4th edn, McGraw-Hill Irwin, Boston, USA.

Booth, A., Roberts, R. & Sikes, J. 2011, 'How strong is your IT strategy?', *McKinsey on Business Technology*, Number 23, Summer 2011, pp. 2–7.

Bughin, J., Chui, M. & Johnson, B. 2012, 'The next step in open innovation', *McKinsey Quarterly*, June 2008, pp. 1–8.

Chui, M. & Fleming, T. 2011, 'Inside P & G's digital revolution', *McKinsey Quarterly*, November 2011, pp. 1–11.

Dumont, C., Kaura, A. & Sunramanian, S. 2012, 'The Faster New World of Health Care', *Strategy+Business*, iss. 66, Spring 2012, pp. 1–3.

Gregersen, H. & Dyer, J. 2012, 'How innovative leaders maintain their edge', Forbes, Sep 5, 2012, Online Available: `http://www.forbes.com/sites/innovatorsdna/2012/09/05/how-innovative-leaders-maintain-their-edge/?utm_source=INSEAD+List&utm_campaign=3f5cd84337-News_Alert_Most_Innovative_Companies&utm_medium=email` (accessed Sep 12, 2012).

Jaruzelski, B. & Dehoff, K. 2008, 'Beyond the borders: the global innovation 1000', *Strategy+Business*, iss. 53, Winter 2008, pp. 1–16.

Jaruzelski, B. & Dehoff, K. 2010, 'The global Innovation 1000: How the top innovators keep winning', *Strategy+Business*, iss. 61, Winter 2010, pp. 1–14.

Jaruzelski, B. & Dehoff, K. 2011, 'The global innovation 1000: Why culture is the key', *Strategy+Business*, iss. 65, Winter 2011, pp. 1–16.

Jaruzelski, B., Holman, R. & Baker, E. 2011, '3M's Open Innovation', *Strategy+Business*, May 30, 2011, Online Available at: `http://www.strategy-business.com/article/00078?gko=121c3` (accessed July 12, 2012).

Jaruzelski, B., Loehr, J. & Holman, R. 2012, 'The global innovation 1000: Making ideas work', *Strategy+Business*, iss. 69, Winter 2012, pp. 1–14.

Kleiner, A. 2012, 'Brand transformation on the Internet', *Strategy + Business*, June 25, 2012, Online Available at: `http://www.strategy-business.com/article/00117?pg=all` (accessed July 20, 2012).

Laudon, K.C. & Laudon, J.P. 2012, Management information systems: Managing the digital firm, 12th edn, Prentice Hall.

Lichtenthaler, U., Hoegl, M. & Muethel, M. 2011, 'Is your company ready for open innovation', *MIT Sloan Management Review*, Vol. 53, No. 1, pp. 45–48.

Manyika, J. 2008, 'Google's views on the future of business: An Interview with CEO Eric Schmidt', *McKinsey Quarterly*, September 2008, Online available at: `https://www.mckinseyquarterly.com/Googles_view_on_the_future_of_business_An_interview_with_CEO_Eric_Schmidt_2229` (accessed Aug 2, 2012).

Manyika, J. 2009, 'Hal Varian on how the Web challenges managers", *McKinsey Quarterly*, January 2009, Online available at: `https://www.mckinseyquarterly.com/Strategy/Innovation/Hal_Varian_on_how_the_Web_challenges_managers_2286` (accessed July 23, 2012).

Mendonca, L. T. & Sutton, R. 2008, 'Succeeding at open-source innovation: An interview with Mozilla's Mitchell Baker', *McKinsey Quarterly*, January 2008, pp. 1–8.

O'Brien, J. A. & Marakas, G. M.2011, *Management Information Systems*, 10th Edition, McGraw-Hill, New York, USA.

Pearlson, K.E. & Saunders, C.S. 2004, *Managing and Using Information Systems: A Strategic Approach*, 2nd edn, Wiley, Danvers.

Pearlson, K. E. & Saunders, C. S. 2010, *Managing and Using Information Systems: A Strategic Approach*, Fourth Edition, John Wiley & Sons, USA.

Rigby, D. 2011, 'The Future of Shopping", *Harvard Business Review*, December 2011, pp. 65-76.

Robert, R & Sikes, J 2008, 'McKinsey global survey results: IT's Unmet potential', *McKinsey Quarterly*, November 2008, pp. 1–9.

Roberts, R. & Sikes, J. 2011, 'How IT is managing new demands: McKinsey Global Survey results', *McKinsey on Business Technology*, Number 22, Spring 2011, pp. 24-33.

Turban, E., King, D., Viehland, D. & Lee, J. 2006, *Electronic Commerce 2006: A Managerial Perspective*, International edn, Prentice Hall, Upper Saddle River, NJ.

Wagstaff, J. 2012, 'Samsung challenge: sold the phone, how to keep the customer', *Reuters*, Online Available at: `http://www.reuters.com/article/2012/09/06/us-samsung-ecosystem-idUSBRE8841J520120906?feedType=RSS&feedName=technologyNews&utm_source=feedburner&utm_medium=feed&utm_campaign=Feed%3A+reuters%2FtechnologyNews+%28Reuters+Technology+News%29` (accessed on Sep 12, 2012).

Wikipedia 2012, Firefox, *Wikimedia Foundation*, Online available at: `http://en.wikipedia.org/wiki/Firefox` (accessed Aug 10, 2012) Economist Intelligence Unit 2005, Business 2010: Embracing the Challenge of Change, Economist Intelligence Unit Ltd, February 2005, pp. 32.

Chapter 3
Information Systems Planning and Evaluation

In this topic we will discuss the importance of alignment between information systems strategy and business strategy, argue the importance of evaluating the performance of information systems initiatives/investments, describe metrics for measuring performance of information systems initiatives/investments, present methods for information systems investment justification, and discuss difficulties associated with justifying information systems investments.

3.1 Strategic Alignment of Information Systems Plan with Business Strategy

Business goals and information systems plans need to be aligned. Information systems plans need to align with business goals and support those goals. However in today's dynamic environment, how can you make strategy and how can you plan when information technologies are changing so rapidly? There is a need to align information systems planning concurrent with strategic planning for a firm, especially in the environment where technologies are changing rapidly and uncertainty is common phenomenon in the market. Some benefits of doing so are (McNurlin & Sprague 2004, pp. 116–117):

- A good planning process helps organisations learn about themselves and promote organisational change and renewal.
- Managing information systems requires planning for changes in business goals, processes, structures, and technologies.
- Good information systems planning can greatly assist organisations' efforts in strategic use of information systems for competitive advantage
- Many information systems projects in organisations have not been successful. One of the important reasons is the lack of proper planning for them.

However IS/IT planning is not an easy task. Some of the reasons suggested by McNurlin & Sprague (2004, pp. 116–117) include:

- Companies need a balanced portfolio of projects.

- Infrastructure development is difficult to fund.
- Responsibility needs to be shared: business planning, not just a technology issue.
- A balanced approach is needed: a balance is needed between (1) top down approach and bottom-up approach and (2) between radical change and continuous improvement.

McNurlin and Sprague (2004, p. 118) state that traditionally strategy formulation has followed a linear process, where (1) business executives created a business plan that described the directions of the business;(2) information systems executives then develop an information systems strategic plan responding to how information systems would support the business plan; and (3) following that an implementation plan was created to address the details of implementation.

McNurlin and Sprague (2004, p. 118) further point out that nowadays the Internet and other technological advances require changing some assumptions that were made about information systems strategy formulation:

- The future cannot be predicted: who predicted the Internet, Amazon, eBay, and Google?
- Information systems do not just support the business anymore: they are an essential platform for and an integral part of the business.
- Top management may not know best: need to look at both internal and external expertise.
- An organisation is not like an army: the industrial era metaphor is not relevant any more.

The new information systems strategic planning process should be a two-way street where, on the one hand, information systems align with business strategies and support planned business operations, while on the other hand information systems also have impacts (or inject input) on the making of business strategy, i.e. by demonstrating information systems-based capabilities and predicting emerging technologies and trends before business strategy is made (McNurlin & Sprague 2004, p. 119). Information systems and the business should stay together rather than the conventional practice of business first and information systems second.

Information systems strategy development should involve business managers leaders while corporate strategy planning should have the input from information systems operation/function. Managers should be educated and be keen in understanding capabilities of new technologies/systems and emerging trends and future directors of information systems, and information systems staff should step into the role of "Business Strategist" (Copper & Nocket 2009). In addition, another critical point for information systems success in the organizations (especially large organizations) is head of information systems operation/function (i.e., chief information officer) should be a member of senior executive team of the organization and most importantly he/she should have a say to the development of business strategies of the organization. Furthermore, organizations need to distinguish strategic and non-strategic dimensions of information systems ((Boochever, Park & Weinberg 2002): information systems infrastructure (i.e., telecommunication networks, network management) are essential but non-strategic information systems while applications such as enterprise resource planning systems, customer relationship management systems, knowledge management systems and supply chain management systems are strategic information systems.

Furthermore, traditional planning at 'start of year' is not good enough anymore. In response to the rapid changes in the market and dramatic advancement in technology, McNurlin and Sprague (2004, p. 116) suggest that there is a need for continuous planning, where there is a need to form a best-available vision of the future upon which to base current decision making. They also point out advanced technology groups should be formed to monitor technology trends and recommend suitable new technology to the organisation, and in large organisations there is also a trend for Chief Information Officers (CIOs) to be part of senior management. Meanwhile the traditional top-down approach of making information systems strategy is becoming more and more irrelevant in the current business context. And both top-down and bottoms up (to truly understand the concerns and needs of end users) elements are essential in achieving effectiveness of IS/IT planning. O'Brien and Marakas (2011, p. 584) suggest a business/information systems planning process, which emphasises a customer and business value focus for developing business strategies and models before information systems strategies and an information systems architecture are developed. They also suggest that components of Business/Information Systems Planning include:

(1) Strategy development: establishing business strategies that support business vision.
(2) Resource management: designing strategic plans for managing or outsourcing information systems resources.
(3) Information Technology Architecture: making strategic information systems choices that reflect a computing architecture designed to support business/information systems initiatives. Architecture includes:
  - Technology platform: including networks, computer systems, system software and integrated enterprise application software.
  - Data resources: consisting of operational and specialised databases.

- Applications architecture: integrated architecture of enterprise-wide systems.
- Information systems organization: organisational structure and management of the IS function.

3.1.1 *Assessing the quality of information systems strategy*

That following a good approach to develop information systems strategy is not sufficient to ensure the ultimate success of well-planned information systems strategy. Good execution is another critical factor, and in fact it can be argued (at least to some extent) sometimes a good execution of third-grade strategy is better than poor execution of first-grade strategy. Another important dimension, which has not been well exposed and practiced, is how to assess the quality of information systems strategy-in other words, many executives have no clear idea of how they can know whether their organizations have a good/strong information systems strategy. Booth, Roberts and Sikes (2011) has contributed in this area by proposing a set of ten tests/questions to help executives (information systems and non-information systems) to judge the quality and rigor of their information systems strategy and plans. Their recommended tests/questions are:

1. Are information systems focusing on beating the competition OR just keeping the lights on (for immediate operational needs and meeting the near-term demands of business units)?
2. Do information systems take a systematic and granular view of required capabilities across the whole organization (understanding critical business processes and delivery demands for different business units and working on synergies across the firm) OR simply assume every part of the business has the same needs?
3. Does information systems strategy take into consideration of potential technology disruptions and emerging trends OR simply stick to the old assumptions?
4. Does information systems strategy factor in flexibility in staffing and budgeting to meet unforeseen situations/changes OR is simply developed from false precision and over-commits to existing programs?
5. Does information systems strategy take a long term view and look at establishing a portfolio including both near-term, well understood projects and larger efforts with potential future value OR is locked into a fixed plan with limited ability to responding changes?
6. Can information systems strategy be effectively translated into clear actions and required resources OR simply sets on vague and non-actionable statements?

7. Does information systems strategy clearly involves non-information systems investments (i.e., process redesign, training, system deployment, change management) OR Does it take an "information systems only" stance?
8. Does information systems strategy win the support of all major stakeholders (internal and external) OR Is it simply pushed by information systems function or/and top management (If information systems strategy has not been discussed and shared with internal (i.e., different business units) and external stakeholders (i.e., partners and customers))?
9. Does information systems strategy pay sufficient close attention to soft factors influencing the success of information systems (i.e., people, relations, structure, culture, management support) OR Does it simply focus on technical issues?
10. Does information systems strategy aim at actively reducing complexity and moving to a simpler and more flexible architecture OR Does it allow the complexity to looks after itself (hope it can fade away automatically)?

3.2 Measuring the Success of Information Systems Initiatives/Investments

When organisations can gain benefits from investing in information technology (Stiroh 2001), there is also a need for organisations to routinely analyse efficiency and effectiveness metrics to measure the performance of information systems projects and justify their information systems investments. The costs of information systems projects have been climbing, many expensive information systems projects have not been completed successfully (typically over the budget and behind the schedule), and many business leaders have perceived information systems as a "blackbox" for investment (Cooper & Nocket 2009) or/and as a pure cost center: a necessary evil for running the business (Alvarez & Raghavan 2010). The worries of business leaders for information systems investments are reasonable, especially given the large scale of annual information systems investments (for example, according to Gartner Inc (cited in Alvarez and Raghavan 2010), in 2009 the worldwide corporate information systems investments were more than US$ 1.3 trillion.

There is an old saying that: 'If you cannot measure it, you cannot manage it'. According to Turban et al. (2006, p. 603) through systematic assessment of their strategic initiatives, organisations can:

(1) Ensure their strategic initiatives are delivering what they are supposed to deliver and apply corrective actions

(2) Determine if their strategic initiatives are still viable in the current environment
(3) Reassess the initial strategy and projects and improve future strategic planning
(4) Identify failing initiatives and projects and causes as soon as possible and avoid the same mistakes/problems for future initiatives/projects.

Meanwhile through effectively managing IS/IT investment benefits, organizations can also achieve such benefits as: (1) better planning; (2) improved relationship between IS/IT and business; (3) better IS/IT investment decisions, and (4) increased realized benefits from IS/IT investments (Peppard, Ward & Daniel 2007). Haag, Baltzan and Phillips (2006, p. 486) point out that by quickly confirming success or immediately identifying corrective actions needed, metrics provide feedback to the firm and can assist senior managers in making better strategic decisions. In the meantime, companies also need to assess the success of information systems projects after they have been completed.

In order to measure the performance of information systems, organisations need to create a set of metrics. Efficiency metrics and Effectiveness metrics are two primary types of information systems measurement metrics. Haag, Baltzan and Phillips (2006, p. 30) suggest that efficiency metrics focus on technology and include throughput, speed, availability, accuracy, Web traffic, and response time. On the other hand, Effectiveness metrics deal with the impact technology has on business processes and activities, concentrate on an organisation's goals, strategies, and objectives, and include usability, customer satisfaction, conversation rates and financial metrics (Haag, Baltzan & Phillips 2006, pp. 30–31). Equipped with effectiveness and efficiency metrics, organizations could constantly review information systems projects and take actions accordingly (including terminating a project if it does not meet the established/agreed metrics).

3.3 Financially Justifying Information Systems Investments

There is an increased demand for financial justification of investing in information systems projects. In many businesses, information systems are a significant part of the annual budget (Pearlson & Saunders 2010, p. 292; Pearlson & Saunders 2004, p. 223). Organisations also don't want to be pushed into buying information systems by the vendors, and they want to spend on information systems projects which can actually produce value. Furthermore, the majority of the businesses will ask their information systems executives to demonstrate the potential value, payback or budget impact of their information systems projects (Pearlson & Saunders 2010, p. 292; Pearlson & Saunders 2004, p. 223). As a result, there exists a clear need to understand and demonstrate the true return of information systems projects.

However measuring and addressing accountability is difficult. Some reasons for this difficulty identified by Pisello (2004) reported in Turban *et al.* (2006, p. 621) include: (1) many company executives lack the knowledge or tools to do return of investment (ROI) calculations; (2) there is a lack of formal processes or budgets in place for measuring ROI; and (3) many company executives do not measure how projects coincide with promised benefits in a timely manner after completion. In addition, very often companies have to make tough decisions on selecting appropriate information systems projects due to funding and resources constraints. Analysis is needed to determine whether funding for information systems investments is appropriate. And in some large companies, and in many public organisations, a formal evaluation of requests for funding of information systems projects is mandated (Turban *et al.* 2006, p. 621).

The five financial metrics of (1) Net present value (NPV – the present value of the stream of net (operating) cash flows from the project minus the project's net investment); (2) Internal rate of return (IRR-the rate at which the NPV of an investment equals zero); (3) Return on investment (ROI – indicates the earning power of a project and is measured by dividing the benefits of a project by the investment); (4) Payback period (PB – the period of time required for the cumulative cash inflows from a project to equal the initial cash outlay; and (5) Total cost of ownership (TCO – consists of the costs, direct and indirect, incurred throughout the life cycle of an asset, including acquisition, deployment, operation, support, and retirement), discussed by Haag, Baltzan and Phillips (2006, pp. 487–492) can be used to justify the information systems investments. Gunasekaran *et al.* (2001) propose that when organisations are deciding on information systems projects, five areas should be addressed:

- Strategic considerations: including strategic objectives of information systems investments, support for corporate strategy, top management support, competitive performance objectives, long term costs and benefits.
- Tactical considerations: including performance indicators, data generation, evaluation methods, security, and senior managers' involvement.
- Operational considerations: including existing information systems, data migration, software, users' attitude, servers, system integration.
- Intangibles: including competitive advantages, services to society, job enrichment, quality improvement, enhanced relations, happier customers, teamwork, good image.

- Tangibles: including financial dimension such as budgets, ROI, revenue, profit, margin and non-financial dimensions such as lead-time, inventory, labour absence, product, defective rates, set-up time.

Alvarez and Raghavan (2010) suggest a very useful road map/process/framework of managing information systems investments, which consists of four steps:

- Identifying required information systems capabilities for supporting organizational strategic priorities/objectives.
- Prioritizing information systems projects as per two criteria of strategic importance and value potential for the investment (i.e., improved performance, reduced costs). By applying these two criteria (we can depict them in two dimensions), there are four types of information systems investments: (1) invest to keep the lights on (low strategic importance and low value potential); (2) invest to sustain high strategic importance and low value potential); (3) invest to refine (low strategic importance and high value potential); and (4) invest to grow (high strategic importance and high value potential). Even though invest to grow is the desirable situation, in reality organizations need to have a balanced portfolio including different types of IS/IT investments to achieve a balance between survival and sustainable growth. The emphasis of matching up with the IS/IT projects with strategic direction and objectives can be seen as taking the approach of demand (for IS/IT) management approach (Cooper and Nocket 2009).
- Deciding the sequence of investment and associated activities (and the flow/plan of the associated activities).
- Working out required support for the approved investment (i.e., cultural & structural fit, top management support).

Another important aspect of managing information systems investments is effective benefit realization management for reasons such as clearer and better information systems planning, improved relations between business and information systems, wiser information systems investments, and increasing the benefits realized from information systems investments (Peppard, Ward & Daniel 2007). One essential element of effective benefit realization of information systems investments is developing an effective benefit realization strategy and successfully implementing benefit realization process (Blick & Quaddus 2003).

Reasons suggested by Turban *et al.* (2006, pp. 624–627) for the difficulties in measuring and justifying information systems investments include:

1. Difficulties in measuring productivity and performance gains:

- Data and data analysis may hide the productivity gains. It is more difficult to measure (i.e. defining input and products) the gains in service industry than in manufacturing industry. And most of the time, the benefits of information systems projects are less tangible than manufacturing products or building plants.
- Productivity gains may be offset by losses in other areas, such as online sales gains may be offset by losses of offline sales.
- Incorrectly defines what is measured, such as productivity gains may not be the same as profit gains.
- Information systems projects may take a few years to show results but many studies do not allow for such a time frame.

2. Difficulties in relating information systems expenditures to organisational performance: Soh and Markus (1995) present a process to examine the relationship between information systems investment and its impact on organisation:
- The relationship between investment and performance is indirect and follow the direction of Information Systems Expenditure >> Information Systems Assets >> Information Systems Impacts >> Organizational Performance.
- Factors such as shared information systems assets and how they are used can impact organisational performance and make it difficult to assess the value of information systems investments.

3. Difficulties in measuring costs and benefits:
- Many costs and benefits of information systems projects are difficult to quantify, especially those intangible costs and benefits. At the same time, information systems are too deeply embedded in most business processes. It is very hard to isolate and measure information systems as a separate element. And nowadays many systems are very complex with multiple layers of hardware, software and networks across various functions and different geographic locations.

Another potential difficulty is the mismatch between company timelines. Strategic planning generally spans one to five years whilst financial planning (working on budgets) just looks at the next financial year. The benefits of information systems projects can be expected over several years or even the entire life of the project. A further difficulty in justifying information systems investments is the knowledge that within a few years of implementation, new systems will make present information systems investments outdated. Organizations thus need to pay close attention to market changes and emerging trends & technologies. Turban *et al.* (2006, p. 622) also point out that justification may not be necessary when (1) the value of the investment is relatively small for the organisation; (2) the relevant data are not available, inaccurate, or too volatile; and (3) the project is mandated – it must be done regardless of the costs and benefits involved.

3.4 Summary

In this chapter, the importance of information systems planning and measuring the performance of information systems initiatives/investments was discussed. Different measurement metrics were reviewed. And some methods for justifying information systems investment and associated difficulties with justifying information systems investments were presented. In the next chapter, we will look at developing and implementing information systems.

Bibliography

Alvarez, E. & Raghavan, S. 2010, 'Road Map to Relevance: How a capabilities-driven information technology strategy can help differentiate your company', *Strategy + Business*, Iss. 61, pp. 1–6.

Blick, G. & Quaddus, M. 2003, *Benefit Realization with SAP: A Case Study*, Graduate School of Business, Curtin University of Technology, Australia, pp. 1–16.

Boochever, J. O., Park, T. & Weinberg, J. C. 2002, 'CEO vs CIO: Can this marriage be saved', *Strategy + Business*, Iss.28, pp. 1–10.

Booth, A., Roberts, R. & Sikes, J. 2011, 'How strong is your IT strategy?', *McKinsey on Business Technology*, Number 23, Summer 2011, pp. 2–7.

Copper, B. & Nocket, K. 2009, 'Toyota's IT Transformation', *Strategy + Business*, Iss. 55, pp. 1–3.

Gunasekaran, A., Love, P.E.D., Rahimi, F. & Miele, R. 2001, 'A Model for Investment Justification in Information Technology Projects', International Journal of Information Management, Vol. 21, pp. 349–364.

Haag, S., Baltzan, p. & Phillips, A. 2006, *Business Driven Technology*, 1st edition, McGraw-Hill Irwin, Boston, USA.

McNurlin, B.C. & Sprague, R.H. 2004, *Information Systems Management in Practice*, 6th edn, Pearson Education, New Jersey.

O'Brien, J. A. & Marakas , G. M. 2011, *Management Information Systems*, 10th Edition, McGraw-Hill, New York, USA.

Pearlson, K.E. & Saunders, C.S. 2004, *Managing and Using Information Systems: A Strategic Approach*, 2nd edn, Wiley, Danvers.

Pearlson, K. E. & Saunders, C. S. 2010, *Managing and Using Information Systems: A Strategic Approach*, Fourth Edition, John Wiley & Sons, USA.

Peppard, J., Ward, J. & Daniel, E. 2007, 'Managing the realization of benefits from IT investment', *MIS Quarterly Executive*, Vol. 6, No. 1, pp. 1–11.

Soh. C. & Markus, L.M. (1995). 'How IT Creates Business Values: A Process Theory Synthesis', *Proceedings of the 16th International Conference on Information Systems*, Amsterdam, Netherlands, pp. 29–41.

Turban, E., King, D., Viehland, D. & Lee, J. 2006, *Electronic Commerce 2006: A Managerial Perspective*, International edn, Prentice Hall, Upper Saddle River, NJ.

Chapter 4
Developing and Implementing Information Systems

In this chapter, we will describe the system approach to problem solving, explain the steps of the systems development life cycle, point out the need for successful project management, change management and risk management, and compare different development approaches organisations can apply.

4.1 Systems Analysis and Design

4.1.1 *The need for system development*

Developing and implementing information systems are very critical to the success of the business. Haag, Baltzan and Phillips (2008, p. 202) stress properly developed information systems can make an organization more flexible and agile. On the other hand, poorly developed and implemented information systems can have damaging effects on business performance (i.e., decreased revenue, increased liabilities, losses in productivity, and damage to brand reputation) and can even cause a business to fail. McKeown (2000, p. 221) states that systems development is needed when:

- potential competition and developments in technology lead to the development of a new system to carry out an existing function
- existing systems are modified to carry out additional functions

a system has to run through its full life cycle(i.e. from Phase 1 of Development to Phase 2 of Effective operational use to Phase 3 of Decline in usefulness) In addition, organisations may need to initiate system development to comply with regulations and policies.

4.1.2 *The system approach*

The system approach can be regarded as a special type of problem solving method based on the scientific method where problems and opportunities are examined in a system context.

O'Brien and Marakas (2011, p. 482) suggest that the system approach, which focuses on 'seeing both the forest and the trees' (system orientation), has the following characteristics:
- Seeing interrelationships among systems rather than linear cause-and-effect chains when events occur
- Seeing process of change among systems rather than discrete snapshots of change whenever change occurs
- Applying a system context: identifying systems, sub-systems, and components of systems.

There are five broad stages in the system approach. These five stages are (O'Brien & Marakas 2011, p. 482):

1. Defining a problem/opportunity using system thinking
2. Developing and evaluating alternative system solutions
3. Selecting the system solution that best meets your requirements
4. Designing the selected system solutions to meet your requirements
5. Implementing and evaluating the success of the designed system.

4.1.3 *The systems development life cycle (SDLC)*

When the system approach to problem solving is applied to the development of information systems solutions to business problems, it can be viewed as a multiple process called information systems development cycle, also known as the systems development cycle (SDLC). Some common types of software development methodologies include: waterfall methodology, rapid application development (RAD) methodology, extreme programming (XP) methodology, and agile development methodology (Haag, Baltzan & Phillips 2008, pp. 204–207).

All software development methodologies use the systems development life cycle (SDLC), which basically covers three major elements of (1) understanding the problem/opportunity; (2) developing information systems solution; and (3) implementing the developed solution, even though the way that they use it differs (Haag, Baltzan & Phillips 2008, p. 460; O'Brien & Marakas 2011, p.486). For example, all projects must have planning and testing phases, however one project might use the waterfall approach and have the planning occur at the beginning of the project and the testing occur at the end. Another project might use the XP method and have small planning and testing phases occurring all the time.

4.1.3.1 *Agile software development*

Agile software development is getting popular among IS/IT programmers and departments. It pushes for fast and iterative development through closely working with end users and allowing continual feedback and refinement. Instead of years of development time for large software development projects, small-scale and more user-focused systems and capabilities can be deployed in a matter of weeks and months (Roberts, Sarrazin & Sikes 2010). Agile software development approach provides more flexible IS/IT capabilities for organizations to deal with changes in the business needs.

4.1.4 *Systems development life cycle (SDLC) models*

Haag, Baltzan and Phillips (2008, pp. 203–204) present a seven-stage system development life cycle, which includes planning phase, analysis phase, design phase, development phase, testing phase, implementation phase, and maintenance phase. Each phase consists of several activities (see Table 4.1).

Table 4.1: Haag, Baltzan & Phillips' (2008) SDLC

Phase of SDLC	Primary Activities
Planning	1. Identify and select the system for development 2. Assess project feasibility 3. Develop the project plan
Analysis	1. Gather business requirements 2. Create process diagrams 3. Perform a buy vs. build analysis
Design	1. Design the IT infrastructure 2. Design system models
Development	1. Develop the IT infrastructure 2. Develop the database and programs
Testing	1. Write the test conditions 2. Perform the system testing
	Continued on next page

Table 4.1 – continued from previous page

Phase of SDLC	Primary Activities
Implementation	1. Write detailed user documentation 2. Determine implementation method 3. Provide training for the system users
Maintenance	1. Build a help desk to support the system users 2. Perform system maintenance 3. Provide an environment to support system changes

(Source: Developed from Haag, Baltzan & Phillips 2008)

O'Brien and Marakas (2011) classify SDLC into five phases of Investigation, Analysis, Design, Implementation, and Maintenance (see Table 4.2). The Implementation stage of O'Brien and Marakas (2011) includes the three phases of development, testing and implementation stated in Haag, Baltzan and Phillips (2008).

Table 4.2: O'Brien and Marakas's (2011) SDLC

Phase of SDLC	Primary Activities
Systems Investigation	1. Identify and select system for development 2. Assess feasibility 3. Develop a project management plan
Systems Analysis	1. Understand current organization and its current systems 2. Analyze information needs of stakeholders 3. Gather functional requirements to meet the information needs
Systems Design	1. Develop specification for hardware, software, people, network, data resources, and associated information products for new system 2. Design logical models of new system

Continued on next page

Table 4.2 – continued from previous page

Phase of SDLC	Primary Activities
Systems Implementation	1. Acquire (or develop) hardware and software 2. Test the new system and convert to the new system 3. Train the users and manage associated change management
Systems Maintenance	1. Conduct post-implementation review 2. Make adjustments to the new systems as needed

(Source: Developed from O'Brien & Marakas 2011)

One important aspect associated with implementing the new system is the conversion process, which is very critical to the success of new system in the organization. There are four conversion approaches and each has its advantages and disadvantages (see Table 4.3). Organizations need to select a conversion approach carefully by weighing its pros and cons, and could adopt the combined approach, such as having pilot approach within phased approach; adopting parallel approach (i.e. keeping the option of going back to the old system until the new system is running smoothly).

Table 4.3: Four conversion approaches

Conversion Approach	Characteristics	Advantages	Disadvantages	Risk
Direct	Simultaneously shutdown old and start new systems	Fast, lower cost	New system may not work	High
Parallel	Run old & new systems at same time	Able to fix problems with new system while old system is in operation	Slower than direct approach, expensive to run both versions, performance problems due to running two systems	Low

Continued on next page

Table 4.3 – continued from previous page

Conversion Approach	Characteristics	Advantages	Disadvantages	Risk
Pilot	Install & test in one part of organisation before installing everywhere	Find and fix problems without affecting entire organisation	Problems with high volumes of transactions may not be found	Moderate
Phased	System installed sequentially at different locations	Requires less installation staff, problems at one location can be fixed before installing elsewhere	Different locations are not using the same version of the system	Moderate

(Source: Developed from McKeown 2000; Marakas & O'Brien 2011)

4.2 Project management, Change Management and Risk Management

A successful system development is backed up by effective project management, which is 'the application of knowledge, skills, tools and techniques to project activities in order to meet or exceed stakeholder needs and expectations from a project' (Haag, Baltzan & Phillips 2008, p. 478). The previously discussed SDLC can be viewed as a specific project management approach, which is a tailored project management approach toward the development and implementation of information systems (O'Brien & Marakas 2011, p. 507). In many circumstances, a project team, consisting of both insiders from different departments and outsiders (i.e. vendors and consultants), will be formed, especially for large and complex systems development and implementations in large organisations. A project manager is needed for the project management team. Haag, Baltzan and Phillips (2008, pp. 479–480) argue while a project manager could be responsible for many tasks, the three primary activities performed by a project manager include choosing strategic projects, setting the project scope, and managing resources and maintaining the project plan.

Haag, Baltzan and Phillips (2008, p. 486) describe some successful project management strategies: (1) establishing project success criteria; (2) developing a solid project plan; (3) dividing large tasks into smaller manageable ones; (4) planning for change and having flexibility; and (5) effectively managing (negative) risks associated with the project. Similarly Nelson (2007) identifies some classic project management mistakes and proposes some relevant solutions. His identified mistakes include (1) poor estimating and/or scheduling the delivery of the project; (2) ineffective stakeholder management; (3) insufficient risk management; (4) insufficient planning; (5) poor quality assurance; (6) weak personnel (no sufficient skills and experiences for the project) and team issues (i.e., difficulties associated with making global teams work effectively as a result of the lack of face-to-face interaction, time-zone differences, cultural differences (including language barriers); and (7) insufficient project sponsorship. He also suggests several solutions/measures to deal with these issue, such as (1) adopting agile development; (2) developing effective communication plan; (3) applying estimate-convergence graph; (4) using joint application development: (5) having comprehensive project chart; (6) establishing project manage office; (7) working on retrospectives; (8) embarking on staged delivery; (9) managing stakeholder assessment; and (10) implementing work breakdown structure. In addition, crafting and executing effective benefits realization strategy (especially for large-scale information systems projects such as ERP system implementations) is essential as well.

Large-scale information systems projects (i.e., more than US$ 15 million) have a tendency to complete behind the schedule, blow the planned budget, and fail to deliver the expected results. A recent joint study by McKinsey & University of Oxford, which surveyed 5,400 large information systems projects, found that on average large projects run 45% over budget and 7% over time, while 56% delivering less value than expected(cited in Bloch, Blumberg & Laartz 2012). The joint study also identified major issues resulting in most project failures: missing focus (i.e., unclear objectives, lack of business focus); content issues (i.e., shifting requirements, technical complexity); skill issues (unaligned team, lack of skills); and execution issues (unrealistic schedule, reactive planning). In addition, the joint study further provided suggestions for project success: managing strategy and stakeholders (looking at such factors as: clear objectives, well-defined business case, alignment of major project scope, minimized & stable project scope, robust vendor contracts with clear responsibilities, executive support); mastering technology and content (looking at such factors as standardized & proven software technology, user involvement to shape solution); building team & capabilities (looking at such factors as experienced project manager, qualified & motivated project team, sustainable mix or internal & external resources); and excelling at project management practices (looking at such factors as reliable estimates & plans, appropriate transparency about project status, proven methodologies & tools).

Introducing new systems into organisations will inevitably result in resistance from the users of the systems. This is quite normal since it is human nature to look at anything new with suspicion. Very often people will ask the question – What is in it for me? As a result, change management, which is defined as 'a set of techniques that aid in evolution, composition, and policy management of the design and implementation of a system' (Haag, Baltzan & Phillips 2008, p. 483), is highly relevant. Good change management can help organisations reduce risks and costs of change and optimise the benefits. The most difficult aspect to handle in change management is dealing with people (in both communication and in culture aspects).

Some guiding principles for change management include (O'Brien and Marakas 2011, p. 472; Jones, Aguirre and Calderone 2004; Wang 2010; The Authors' Own Knowledge):

- Emphasizing the importance of addressing "human side" side systematically and effectively answering the question of "What is in it for me": The most difficult aspect to handle in change is to do with people. Resisting to changes is human being's nature. Organizations need to make sure people understand the benefits of changes to the organization as well as to them and the risks of not making changes. At the same time, people's needs have to be looked after.
- Focusing on top management and developing leadership: Leaders should be initiators of the change, lead the change management, take responsibilities for the change management, and set good examples for people to follow.
- Creating change vision: understanding strategic vision, creating compelling story, and make vision comprehensive and operational.
- Defining change strategy: assessing change readiness, choosing best change configuration, and putting change governance into place.
- Involving people from different parts and different levels of the organization: better understanding and better education of the change will be made easier.
- Building and sustaining commitment: forming teams, managing stakeholders, communicating effectively and sufficiently, dealing with resistance, disseminating best practices and knowledge/skills, and acknowledging achievements in every possible public opportunity.

- Managing individual's performance: organizations need to clearly and honestly communicate to individuals regarding what is expected of them and how they will be measured. And once success and failure metrics and incentives/penalties are established they should be properly followed. Organizations also need to realign certain roles to ensure people stick to the change and new approach/process.
- Realizing business benefits: building business case and constantly quantifying/tangiblizing benefits.
- Developing required culture: identifying the culture gap and implementing required cultural changes.
- Adjusting structure: identifying and implementing necessary changes to organizational structure to embrace the change.
- Preparing for the unexpected: it is very rare that a change management program goes completely according to the plan-the only certainty is the uncertainty-as a result of some unexpected internal and external influences. Organizations need to continually assess the progress and performance of the change management program and deal with the unexpected effectively in a timely manner. In addition, they need to have risk mitigation measures in place to ensure minimum disruption to the business during the change management process.

Another important factor having impact on the success of proposed systems development is project risk, which is 'an uncertain event or condition that, if it occurs, has a positive or negative effect (in Chinese the risk (described in two characters) means both danger/threat and opportunity) on a project (Haag, Baltzan & Phillips 2008, p. 484). However in reality, while we talk about the (project) risk, we normally refer to negative side of the risk. Risks could come from inside (i.e., the withdrawal of support by the top management, the insufficient allocated resources, key people leaving the project suddenly) outside (i.e., changes in the industry standards, new regulations, and competitors' move/advantages in the similar/same projects) of the organization. Just like dealing with any other types of risks, an effective process/framework should be put into place. A simple framework of project risk management can be viewed as: identifying the risk>>quantifying the risks (probably and the impact)>>developing and implementing risk management solutions>>constantly assessing the performance of implemented solutions and making required adjustments/change. Meanwhile effective risk management practices are not common phenomenon for many organizations, and it has only been in the last decade that risk management has been seriously considered as part of managerial responsibilities.

4.3 Internal Development, Outsourcing, Acquisition and Use of Application Service Providers

When organisations are developing new systems, they face several choices:

- Internal development.
- Outsourcing.
- Acquisition – purchase off the shelf.
- Use of application service providers (ASP).

Each of them has its own advantages and disadvantages (see Table 4.4).

Table 4.4: Comparison of Development Options

Development Options	Advantages	Disadvantages
Internal Development	Competitive advantage Complete control over final system Building technical skill and functional knowledge of developers	Requires dedicated effort of in-house staff Development can be slow Costs may be higher than working with other approaches System may not work when completed or may not provide desired functionality
		Continued on next page

Table 4.4 – continued from previous page

Development Options	Advantages	Disadvantages
Outsourcing	Cost savings Ease of transition to new technologies Better strategic and business focus Better management of information systems staff – vendor has the knowledge and skills in effectively managing information systems staff Handling peaks with greater capacity of vendor Consolidating data centers is a very difficult task to be done by an internal group Infusing cash via selling equipment to the outsourcing vendor	Loss of control High switching cost Lack of technological innovation Loss of strategic advantage Reliance on outsourcer Security and reliability Evaporation of cost saving, i.e. perceived costs may never be realised due to factors such as out-of-date processes, costs arising from software upgrades, unspecified growth and new technologies not anticipated in the contract. And some savings may be hard to measure
Acquisition	Purchasing of a complete system from a vendor Packages ranging from office suite to functional information systems to enterprise systems (i.e., ERP systems) Fastest approach of all	Little competitive advantage Must accept functionality of purchased system May not integrate well with existing systems May require modification to meet needs

Continued on next page

Table 4.4 – continued from previous page

Development Options	Advantages	Disadvantages
Use of Application Service Providers (ASPs)	Firms, especially SMEs, will enjoy the benefit of less need for dedicated internal information systems staff Saving money on internal infrastructure and initial capital layouts Some companies find it easier to 'rent' software from an ASP and avoid the problems associated with installing, operating and maintaining complex systems like ERP Easier to walk away from unsatisfactory systems solutions Quicker to respond to market with applications available from ASP	Less control over the applications, i.e. when application is upgraded or how access to it is facilitated Applications from ASPs tend to address routine problems, and there is not much attention in how a particular problem the organisation is facing is addressed ASP solutions tend to be rather generic, i.e. normally allowing only 20% customisation for any given company

(Source: developed from McKeown 2000, p. 251; Perlason & Saunders 2010, pp. 192–194; Hoffer *et al.* 2005, pp. 32–33, 38–39, 40–41)

ASP is a business that delivers and manages applications and computer services from a remote computer centre to multiple users via the Internet or a private network (Laudon & Laudon 2005, p. 227). Users pay for the use of software through a subscription, license or per use basis. It normally involves using an outside company to perform the information systems development on your behalf (Laudon & Laudon 2005, p. 227). We will have more discussion on outsourcing in chapter 10 looking at information systems operation/function management.

So how can an organisation choose the best system development approach? Organisations can choose any of the four development approaches after evaluating advantages and disadvantages of different development approaches and taking into consideration their organisational circumstances and requirements. Alternatively a combined system development approach also can be pursued, i.e. using a prototype as part of the traditional life cycle, using a small application package as a prototype, adopting aspects of a traditional life cycle to purchasing an application package, and adding a user development component to the traditional life cycle. On a related note, for small firms and some medium enterprises they also can try online outsourcing service providers such as freelancer.com, which aims to become the "the eBay of jobs".

4.4 Summary

In this chapter, we developed an understanding of the system approach to problem solving and its application in developing information systems-the systems development life cycle (SDLC). Details of steps of the SDLC were reviewed. We also covered project management that plays an important role in the success of systems development. A comparison between different systems development approaches was also presented. We will now move to the discussion of information systems infrastructure management in the next chapter.

Bibliography

Bloch, M., Blumberg, S. & Laartz, J. 2012, "Delivering large-scale IT projects on time, on budget, and on vlaue', *McKinsey Technology Office*, October 2012, pp. 1–6.

Haag, S., Baltzan, P. & Phillips, A. 2008, *Business Driven Technology*, 2nd edn, McGraw-Hill Irwin, Boston, USA.

Hoffer, J.A. , George, J.F. & Valacich, J.S. 2005, *Modern Systems Analysis and Design*, 4th edn, Prentice Hall.

Jones, J., Aguirre, D. & Calderone, M. 2004, "10 Principles of Change Management", *Strategy + Business*, April 2004, pp. 1–5.

McKeown, P. 2000, *Information Technology and the Networked Economy*, Thomson Learning, Boston.

Nelson, R.R. 2007, "IT Project Management: Infamous Failures, Classic Mistakes, and Best Practices", *MIS Quarterly Executive*, Vol. 6, No. 2, pp. 67–78.

O'Brien, J. A. & Marakas , G. M. 2011, *Management Information Systems*, 10th Edition, McGraw-Hill, New York, USA.

Pearlson, K. E. & Saunders, C. S. 2010, *Managing and Using Information Systems: A Strategic Approach*, Fourth Edition, John Wiley & Sons, USA.

Roberts, R. Sarrazin, H. & Sikes, J. 2010, 'Reshaping IT management for turbulent times', *McKinsey on Business Technology*, Number 21, pp. 2–9.

Wang, K. W. 2010, 'Creating Competitive Advantage with IT Architecture', *McKinsey on Business Technology*, Number 18, Winter 2010, pp. 18–21.

Chapter 5
Managing Organization's Knowledge Resources

In this chapter, we will define data, information and knowledge; explain database, data warehousing and data mining; discuss the phenomenon of Big Data; and look at knowledge management and knowledge management systems.

5.1 Data, Information and Knowledge

Even though in reality we tend to use data, information and knowledge interchangeably for the purpose of convenience, it is essential to define and distinguish data, information and knowledge before discuss managing organization's knowledge assets. While there exist no universal definitions on these terms, we view data as "raw figures and simple facts" (i.e., 180, 180cm) and information as "processed data and data with meaning" (i.e., height-180cm). And we reckon knowledge (i.e., Jun Xu's height is 180cm) can only be obtained through learning, practising and doing and is normally sitting on human's brains (yours' or others').

Meanwhile we also take the view that knowledge can be basically divided into two categories: tacit knowledge and explicit knowledge (Polanyi, 1962, 1967; Nonaka & Takeuchi, 1995; Spender, 1996; Alavi & Leidner, 2001; Leonard & Sensiper, 1998). Some common applications of tacit knowledge are problem solving, problem finding, and prediction and anticipation (Leonard & Sensiper, 1998). Tacit knowledge consists of two dimensions: cognitive and technical elements (Nonaka & Takeuchi, 1995). The cognitive dimension of tacit knowledge refers to 'mental models', which assist human beings in interpreting and understanding the world around them; individuals' perspectives, beliefs, and opinions are some examples of tacit knowledge (Nonaka & Takeuchi, 1995). The technical element of tacit knowledge includes things such as know-how, crafts, and skills (Nonaka & Takeuchi, 1995). Tacit knowledge is personal and context-specific; therefore, it is more difficult to formalize and communicate (Nonaka & Takeuchi, 1995). In contrast with tacit knowledge's subjective nature, explicit knowledge is more objective and generally can be codified or documented in a formal or systematic format (Nonaka & Takeuchi, 1995), and other people's tacit knowledge is explicit knowledge for you when they are presented to you in the codified and documented formats. Information in databases, libraries, and the internet are some examples of explicit knowledge. Tacit knowledge has much higher value than explicit knowledge since people always know more than they can tell (Sveiby, 1997, p. 34; Moody & Shanks, 1999). Furthermore, in order to apply explicit knowledge in practice, it must be converted to tacit knowledge (Moody & Shanks, 1999). For example, students have to understand the knowledge (i.e., the concepts, definitions, theories, formulas) they learn in the classroom and books before they can apply them to interpret, understand, and solve the problem in reality.

5.2 Database, Data Warehouse and Data Mining

While we use the name of databases, they actually are technologies and applications for managing (including organizing, storing, and accessing) data, information (processed data and data with meaning), and knowledge (i.e., codified and documented version of lessons learned, past projects, experiences). In practice, we very often use data and information interchangeably while we are talking about data resources and data management.

Data/Information is very valuable to organisations. They need information for everything from their daily operation to crafting strategies (Haag, Baltzan & Phillips 2008, p. 60). Effective management of data in today's Big Data Era where massive volume of data and information is available is critical to the success and survival of the organization. For example, according to Harvard Business Review (June 2010): a typical car contains about 2,000 components, 30,000 parts, and 10 million lines of software codes.

5.2.1 *Database*

In the past, different functional areas and groups developed their own files independently. Traditional file environments create problems such as data redundancy and inconsistency, program-data dependence, inflexibility, poor security, and lack of data sharing availability (Laudon & Laudon 2012, p. 240).

Database technology can provide solutions to many of the problems of a traditional file processing and data organisation approach. A database is a collection of data organised to service many applications efficiently by storing and managing data (Laudon

& Laudon 2005, p. 238). Haag, Baltzan and Phillips (2008, p. 68) point out that benefits of database technology for businesses include: increased flexibility, increased scalability, reduced information redundancy (duplication), increased information integrity (quality), and increased information security. A single database can serve multiple applications. A single database can serve multiple applications and allow an organisation to easily pull out all the information for different purposes. For example, instead of storing employee's data for personnel, payroll and benefits in separate files (or in different places or even in separate information systems), the organisation could establish a human resources database (Laudon & Laudon 2005, p. 238).The database management system (i.e. Microsoft Access) is a special software, which permits an organization to centralize data, manage them efficiently, and provide access to the stored data by application programs. Through data management system users and application programs can interact with a database. There are many different database models of how to organise information in a database, including hierarchical, network, relational, multi-dimensional and object-oriented databases. The hierarchical database is used for structured, routine types of transaction processing and is organised in a treelike manner (i.e. looking like a family tree and an organisational chart) (Laudon & Laudon 2005, p. 238). Within each record, data elements are organised into pieces of records called segments. The top level of segment is called root. An upper segment is logically linked to a lower segment in a parent–child (children) relationship.

A hierarchical database is used to model one-to-many relationships, which must be specified in advance. It is complex, not flexible, difficult to modify and doesn't support ad hoc requests well (Laudon & Laudon 2005, p. 243). The network database structure is even more complex than the hierarchical model and depicts many to many relationships, which must be specified in advance as well. While the former is more flexible, it doesn't readily support ad hoc requests (Laudon & Laudon 2005, p. 243). Both of them are older logical database models. The relational model databases store data elements in simple tables and are able to link data elements from various tables. They are very supportive of ad hoc requests but slower at processing large amounts of data than hierarchical or network models. They are more flexible and easier to maintain than hierarchical and network models (Laudon & Laudon 2005, p. 257). The relational database model stores information in the form of logically related two-dimensional tables. Entities, entity classes, attributes, primary keys, and foreign keys are all fundamental concepts included in the relational database model (Laudon & Laudon 2005, p. 240).

The multi-dimensional database is a variation of the relational model. Compared to normal relational databases that store data in simple two-dimensional tables, the multidimensional database stores information in cubes and cubes within cubes and is used for on-line analytical processing (OLAP) applications (manipulating and analysing large volumes of data from multiple perspectives) (O'Brien & Marakas 2011, p. 185). The object-oriented database use objects, which can be automatically retrieved and shared, to store both data (i.e., customers' bank accounts) and the procedures acting on the data (i.e., actions such as checking balance, charging interests). The object-oriented database also supports inheritance. Inheritance refers to new objects that can be automatically created by replicating some or all of the characteristics of one or more parent objects (O'Brien & Marakas 2011, pp. 185). Compared to conventional data base structures (including the relational model) that are not very good at dealing with multimedia or graphical data, the object-oriented data model is a key technology for storing multi-media or graphical based information, especially for web-based applications (Laudon & Laudon 2005, p. 257). It is good for complex, high-volume applications. Many computer-aided design (CAD) applications have adopted object-oriented databases. On the other hand, although object-oriented databases have the capacity to store more complex types of information than relational databases, they can be relatively slower compared to relational databases while dealing with large numbers of transactions. A hybrid object-relational database can combine the capabilities of both relational model for traditional information and object-oriented model for multimedia information (Laudon & Laudon 2012, p. 245; O'Brien & Marakas 2011, p.187).

In the case of enterprise systems (i.e., enterprise resource planning systems), there is centralised database (also called backbone or central repository), which can be used by a single processor (i.e. mainframe computer) or by multiple processes (i.e. mini-computers/mid-range computers) in a client-server network. A database can be distributed, and there are alternative ways of distributing a database. For example, the database in the headquarter can be partitioned so that each remote processor has the necessary data to serve its own local needs, and it can also be replicated at all remote locations (Laudon & Laudon 2005, p. 246).

Organisations usually end up having several databases. Sharing and organising information sitting in multiple databases could be very time-consuming and inefficient if there is no integration across multiple databases in different information systems across various departments/functions. Haag, Baltzan and Phillips (2006, p. 71) introduce two primary methods of integrating information across multiple databases:

- Forward integration – takes information entered into a given system and sends it automatically to all downstream systems and processes.
- Backward integration – takes information entered into a given system and sends it automatically to all upstream systems and processes.

Meanwhile as an important part of online operations, organisations need to link their internal databases to the web. Fortunately, many middleware and other software products are available in the market to help access organisations' legacy systems through the web(i.e. searching product information online from your home computers).

5.2.2 *Data warehousing and data mining*

Technologies such as data warehousing and data mining allow organisations to gain vast amounts of business intelligence. A data warehouse is a single, server-based data repository that allows centralised analysis, security, and control over the data while data mart is a small data warehouse designed for a strategic business unit (SBU) or a department – it is a lower-cost and scaled-down version. Data warehouses support reporting and query tools, store current and historical data, and consolidate data for management analysis and decision-making (Laudon & Laudon 2012, p. 252). A data warehouse extracts current and historical data from both internal (i.e., current data including operational data, customer data, manufacturing/production data, and historical data) and external data sources (i.e., competitor information, regulations, market changes, consumer insights, and other information from strategic alliances, partners and research agencies) and reorganises collected data/information into a centralised database for management reporting and analysis via various tools (i.e. queries & reports, online analytic processing (OLAP), data mining).

The primary purpose of data warehouses (and data marts) is to perform analytical processing or OLAP (Haag, Baltzan & Phillips2008, p. 81). The insights into organisational information that can be gained from analytical processing are instrumental in making critical business decisions (i.e. setting strategic directions and goals) (Laudon & Laudon 2012, p. 253).

Data mining is a major use/application of data warehouse. Information in data warehouses is analysed to reveal hidden correlations, patterns, and trends, which involves sifting through an immense amount of data to discover previously unknown patterns (O'Brien & Marakas 2011, p. 200). Through data mining, firms can search for valuable business information and business opportunities. Online analytical processing (OLAP) is another important data analysis method and mining tool, and it supports manipulation and real-time analysis of large volumes of data from multiple dimensions and perspectives (O'Brien & Marakas 2011, p. 201).

Databases normally contain information in a series of two-dimensional tables, which means that you can only ever view two dimensions of information at one time. In a data warehouse, information is multi-dimensional, and it contains layers of columns and rows (Haag, Baltzan & Phillips2008, p. 83). Each layer in a data warehouse represents information according to an additional dimension. Dimensions could include such things as products, promotions, stores, category, region, stock price, date, time, and even the weather. The ability to look at information from various dimensions can add tremendous business insight (i.e., identifying trends in spending according to age, sex, marital status and postcode). An organisation must maintain high-quality information in the data warehouse. It is very important to ensure the cleanliness of information throughout an organisation. Without high-quality information the organisation will be unable to make good business decisions. A common catch-cry is GIGO – garbage in, garbage out. Organisations can adopt information cleansing and scrubbing, which is 'a process that weeds out and fixes or discards inconsistent, incorrect, or incomplete information' (Haag, Baltzan & Phillips 2008, p. 84) to enhance the quality of information. Meanwhile organizations need to effectively deal with sources of poor quality information, prevention is one of the most effective approaches for enhancing the quality of the information. Some sources of low quality information include: (1) customers intentionally entering inaccurate information to protect their privacy; (2) information from different systems that have different information entry standards and formats; (3) call centre operators enter abbreviated or erroneous information by accident or to save time; and (4) third party and external information contains inconsistencies, inaccuracies, and errors (Haag, Baltzan & Phillips 2008, p. 388).

5.3 The Phenomenon of Big Data

Gathering and analysing large (or very large)-scale data is quickly becoming popular organizations for reasons such as large volume data from multiple channels and various sources, the need for better understanding customers, and the tangible benefits of gaining competitive advantages by doing this (i.e., the success of Amazon, Google) (Bughin, Livingston & Marwaha 2011). Big data can be defined as "data sets whose size is beyond the ability of typical database software tools to capture, store, manage and analyse" (Manyika *et al.*

2011, p. 1). Big data is different with traditional concept of data in four perspective (Dijcks 2012; Brow, Chui and Manyika 2011).

- Bigger volume: in 2010 enterprises and consumers stored 13 exabytes (1 exabytes = 1,024 petabytes = $1,024 \times 1,0124 = 1.049$ million terabytes = $1,024 \times 1,024 \times 1,024 = 1.074$ billion gigabytes) of new data on devices and the projected annual growth in global data generated is 40% (just imaging the information produced by more than 4 billion mobile phones, by 30 million network sensor nodes, social networks-do you know there are more than 30 billion piece of content (photos, notes, blogs, web links, and news stories) shared on Facebook every month and 2.9 billion hours of video are watched at Youtube every month?). Ericsson estimates (cited in Dutta, Bilbao-Osorio & Geiger (2012, p. 3)) there will be more than 50 billion connected devices in the world by 2020. Have you imagined to live in a yotta world (1,000 trillion gigabytes data and your every move will be digitized and added to the data flow of the world) (Siegele 2012). According to EMC/IDC Digital Universe Study 2011 (cited in Siegele 2012), Global digital data will reach 2,720 exabytes by the end of 2012, and 7,920 exabytes by the end of 2015. It is said more data were created between 2008 and 2011 than in all history before 2008 (Biggs *et al.* 2012, p. 48). In the past, data storage was expensive and a lot of data have been thrown away. However the price of storage is dropping significantly, according to Forrest Research (cited in Siegele 2012), by 2020, storing a petabyte data will only cost US$ 4.
- Higher velocity: for example even at 140 characters per tweet, Twitter generated data volume is large than 8 terabytes per day as a result of high velocity or frequency. And it is reported (cited in Conway 2012) 90% of the world's data are generated in the last two years.
- More data variety: including traditional and non-traditional data and structured and unstructured data (i.e., social media data)-it is estimated that 95% of the world data is unstructured data, which makes big data more meaningful and challenging (Oracle 2012). Gartner projects (cited in SAP AG 2012) in the future 80% of enterprise data (from both traditional and non-traditional sources) will be unstructured .
- Higher economic value: huge financial gains can be realized via Big Data via more powerful and accurate decision-making and thus significantly improving business operations and organizational performance. The examples of financial value of big data will be discussed in the following text.

Big Data could exist in various formats (including video, image, audio, text/numbers), and include various types of data, including (1) traditional enterprise data (i.e., customer, transaction, operation information), machine-generated/sensor data (i.e., call details records, weblogs, information from smart meters, manufacturing sensors, equipment logs), and social data (i.e., information from blogs (including micro-blogging sites such as Twitter), social networks). Start-up firms like Lexalytics and Klout have been established for understanding social data (Dijcks 2012). We are in the big data era for reasons such as the cheaper and cheaper data devices (i.e., for US$ 600 you can buy a disk that can store all of the world's music (Brow, Chui and Manyika 2011)), the wide adoption of mobile phones and other mobile devices, and the great connectedness as a result of the availability of extensive networks across the globe.

Big Data could create value for organizations in several ways (Manyika *et al.* 2011, pp. 5-6): (1) creating transparency and improving efficiency via more easy access to more data across the organization; (2) improving productivity and organizational performance through quicker, deeper and more accurate discovery, prediction and analysis; (3) better segmentation with more tailored customization actions; (4) better (automation) support in decision making; (5) enhancing existing products and services and creating new ones through better understanding customers' needs and stronger capabilities in identifying opportunities for new products and services; and (6) becoming a key basis of competition and growth through the use of Big Data for organizations. Specifically Big Data could bring huge financial value to various sectors, for example (Brow, Chui and Manyika 2011; Manyika *et al.* 2011, p. 8):

- US$ 300 billion value per year to US health care sector
- More than 60% net margin increase to US retail sector
- EUR€ 250 billion value per year to Europe public sector administration
- Up to 50% decrease in product development and assembly costs to manufacturing sector
- US$ 100 billion and 700 billion for service providers and end users for the sector of global personal location data
- Huge benefits to sports industry?! -have you watched the popular movie of Moneyball? (Stafford 2012; Lohr 2012), and many others.

Some notable examples of using big data for competitive advantages include: Google, Amazon, Apple, Zipcar, and Netflix. Hagström & Gill (2012, p. 102) point out that the combination of hyper-connectivity, Big Data, and powerful analytics, has enhanced organizational ability to know dialogue, and innovate. In association with the big data phenomenon, there is a shortage of people who have required skills to deal with big data. For example, it is reported the U.S. alone faces a shortage of 140,000 to 190,000 people with deep analytical skills and 1.5 million data-savvy (being able to analyse Big Data and make decisions from Big Data) managers which are equivalent to 50 to 60% gap in supply of required talent (Manyika *et al.* 2011, p. 3; Brow, Chui and Manyika 2011). It can be assumed in the future titles/positions such as "data strategist" , "data scientist", "chief data officer", "data expert", "data specialist", "data technology officer/expert/specialist", "business intelligence (which arguably has more emphasis on using Big Data for deciosn making) specialist", and similar titles, will become common terms for organizations. A more general term of "digital workforce" (Chui & Fleming 2011) has been suggested in recent years, and it includes people with different skills (from programming, computing modelling simulation, data analysis to analytical thinking and many others) for the current digital economy (also called knowledge economy). In addition, for knowledge workers (coined by Peter Drucker) such skills as organizing, accessing, processing, visualizing, understanding, analysing & extracting the value from (large volume) information available in the organization are essential for doing their tasks effectively in the 21st century (Manyika 2009).

Meanwhile some techniques for analysing big data include: A/B testing, Association rule learning, Classification, Cluster analysis, Crowdsourcing, Data fusion and data integration, Data mining, Ensemble learning, Genetic algorithms, Machine learning, Natural language processing, Neural networks, Network analysis, Optimization, Pattern recognition, Predictive modelling, Regression, Sentiment analysis, Signal processing, Spatial analysis, Supervised learning & unsupervised learning, Simulation, Time series analysis, Visualisation, and many others (Manyika *et al.* 2011, pp. 27–31). Some technologies and applications for Big Data are: Big table, Data warehouse, Cassandra, Cloud computing, Distribute system, Dynamo, Google file system, HBasem, Hadpoop, MapReduce, Metadata, Stream processing, Visualisation, and many others (Manyika *et al.* 2011, pp. 31–33).

On top of required techniques & technologies and talent to take advantage of the potential big data, organizations also need to (1) put in place appropriate data policies (especially addressing data sourcing, accessing and disseminating issues and critical but complex (as a result of the size and the sources of data) data security and privacy issues); (2) make necessary organizational adjustments (including structural and cultural changes, end user education); and (3) ensure top management's skills and support for big data use in the organization. Meanwhile the data quality is one of the most critical factors (if not the most critical factor) for using big data for decision making, in order to avoid the problem of "Garbage in and Garbage out", organizations need to work hard on the sources of the data (sources/data partners must be reliable) and on the acquisition/collection of data (i.e., right questions and research design; good understanding of data constraints; and ensuring real-time or timely data) (Chui & Fleming 2011).

However while the huge potential and benefits are recognized, its role and influence should not be overstated. It should be remembered that "human beings are decision-makers not the machine and the big data, they are there to support us to make better decision". Big data could make our decision making process more scientific (Lohr 2012), but the role of our experience and intuition, which is impossible (or extremely hard) for the machine to emulate and acquire, should never be diminished.

5.4 Knowledge Management and Knowledge Management Systems

Knowledge management is "an approach to adding or creating value by more actively leveraging the know-how, experience, and judgment [that] reside within and, in many cases, outside of an organization" (Ruggles, 1998, p. 80). The above definition highlights important elements of knowledge management. The know-how aspect of knowledge management emphasizes explicit knowledge, which can be easily captured and codified (Bonner, 2000). On the other hand, the experience and judgment aspects of knowledge management reflect tacit or implicit knowledge, which is difficult to capture and formalize (Bonner, 2000). The definition also emphasizes that the primary purpose of knowledge management is to add or create value. Knowledge management systems such as intranets, best practice databases, corporate knowledge directories, corporate information portals, knowledge networks and maps and other applications (i.e., online communities, social networks, internal wikis, internal prediction markets, internal Google-type search engines, blogs, discussion boards, feedback forums, online live communication systems, virtual organizations & teams), can also be used to support and enhance knowledge management activities and facilitate the sharing of both tacit and explicit knowledge (Alavi & Leidner 2001; The Authors' Own Knowledge).

There are four modes of tacit and explicit knowledge creation processes (Nonaka & Takeuchi 1995). The four processes are: socialisation, externalisation, combination, and internalisation (see Figure 5.1).

Socialisation refers to the conversion of tacit knowledge to tacit knowledge that is hidden knowledge and hard to communicate, such as knowledge sharing among individuals through face-to-face contact such as interviews, focus group, conversations in the

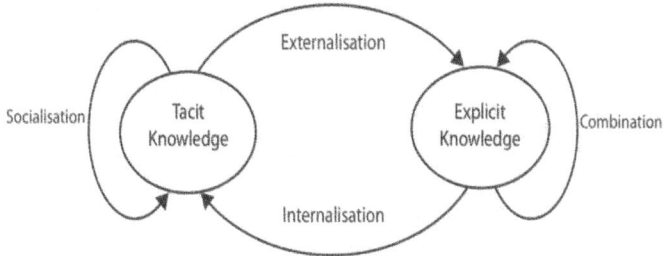

Fig. 5.1 Four knowledge creation processes
(Soruce: adapted from Bolloju *et al.* 2002)

lunch time and coffee/tea break, on-the-job training, master-fellow-relationships, formal and informal networks, and brainstorming. In this knowledge creation process, information systems can be useful in connecting people and creating and sustaining knowledge communities through teleconferencing technologies, including desk-top videoconferencing tools; online live communication systems and virtual organizations and teams; and internal knowledge marketplaces, predication markets, talent marketplaces (Junnakar & Brown 1997, Bryan & Joyce 2005; The Authors' Own Knowledge).

Externalisation is the process of converting tacit knowledge to explicit knowledge in the form of metaphors, analogies, hypothesis, and models, such as articulating tacit knowledge, such as experience, insight, judgment, problem solving skills, obtained through observation, imitation, and practice into the format that can be used for future purpose and by who need it. The creation of explicit knowledge can be dramatically enhanced by information systems including groupware tools and electronic mail as well as wikis, blogs, discussion boards, feedback forums, and virtual organizations and teams (Junnakar & Brown 1997, The Authors' Own Knowledge).

Combination is the creation of new explicit knowledge for individuals through activities of sharing, combining, organising, and processing discrete pieces of and different bodies of explicit knowledge (i.e., information through meetings & telephone conversations, information in the documents, information in the common databases, and information from electronic communication systems).Information systems such as intranets as well as internal wikis, blogs, discussion boards, feedback forums, internal Google-type search engines, internal predication markets, internal eBay type knowledge auction sites, have enabled the paperless forms of explicit to explicit knowledge transfer (Junnakar & Brown 1997; The Authors' Own Knowledge).

Internalisation is a process in which explicit knowledge is absorbed and becomes part of tacit knowledge. This process regards the activities of applying knowledge in practice and reflects the concept of learning by doing (i.e. internalising the new or shared explicit knowledge through hands-on practice). Also documented knowledge can be helpful in this process, such as learning from best practice databases. Applications such as data mining tools, OLAP, internal Google-type search engines, internal predication markets, internal eBay type knowledge auction sites, for enhancing decision-makers' ability to make sense out of explicit information, especially in the presence of complex sets of data, can be very effective in this regard (Junnakar & Brown 1997; The Authors' Own Knowledge).

As demonstrated in the above discussion, information systems and information technology provides essential roles and is an important enabler of knowledge management and knowledge sharing process. One related point is the discussion brought by Davenport (2010). He argues that even though there are a lot of tools available for managing knowledge, the actual information needs of knowledge workers vary and organizations should then provide them with appropriate systems in line with their tasks. He suggests there are four type of knowledge workers (by looking at the two dimensions of level of interdependence and complexity of work) requiring different kinds of support technologies/applications:

- Transaction model (low level of interdependence and low complexity of work): knowledge workers of this category mainly deal with individual and routine tasks, and need more structured-provision tools (i.e., work flow management systems, document management systems, content management systems, case management systems, business-rules or algorism to automate decisions, and business process management or monitoring systems), which have certain control of how knowledge workers get information and do job tasks (on the contrary, free access means knowledge workers can use any tools organizations can provide. The concern here is knowledge workers may know how to use the tools but may not have the skills for using (i.e., how to use different data sources for decision making and how to use different analytics tools), or for sharing the knowledge.
- Integration model (high level of interdependence and low level of complexity of work): knowledge workers under this category normally involve in collaborative groups but systematic and repeatable work, and need some free-access tools (i.e., e-mail and collaborative tools for communications) or/and semi-structured-provision tools (i.e., applications for joint-design, joint-development).

- Expert model (low level of interdependence and high complexity of work): knowledge workers of this kind mainly deal with judgment-oriented work and need to apply their expert knowledge to tasks or problems, and they typically need free access tools (i.e., telephone/video/online conferencing, virtual teams, wikis, social media, online chatting, e-mail systems) to deliver their knowledge sitting in the brain. Organizations also need to apply some structured-provision tools (i.e., expert systems) to record and automate their expertise.
- Collaboration model (high level of interdependence and high complexity of work): Knowledge workers of this type usually deal with iterative and unstructured work and depend on deep expertise across multiple function, and they typically need free access tools (i.e., group decision support systems, collaborative tools, telephone/video/online conferencing, virtual teams, online chatting, wikis, social media, email systems) to work on major plans and big ideas). But structured-provision tools (i.e., best practices & lessons learned databases, internal wikis) for knowledge reuse.

Knowledge sharing is possible in all four knowledge creation processes. The difference is in their focus (tacit, explicit, or both) and the required facilitation and support by information systems. However, resistance to knowledge sharing is probably part of human nature, especially when we believe that knowledge is power and that hidden knowledge can lead to prestige and job security (since only I know, and no one else knows; so they need me). When people are asked to share their knowledge, one question they always ask is: 'What's in it for me?. In addition, people may be reluctant to share their research and data for the following two primary reasons: (1) the fear of being criticized for possible errors and weaknesses and (2) the fear of losing the advantages arising from sharing what they know (Hubbard & Little 1997).

To foster knowledge creation and encourage collaboration and knowledge sharing, we need to take a holistic approach and take into consideration of various related factors. A good example of effectively managing knowledge is Southern Cross University's Doctor of Business Administration (DBA) program. Knowledge is important to everyone in today's knowledge-based economy, and academics will be among those who view knowledge as a very important resource since they are knowledge professionals who engage heavily in creating and delivering knowledge products (publications) and services (lectures, presentations, seminars, supervision, theses examinations), and whose performance appraisals are very much related to these knowledge products and services. For research students, similar issues will come up as they spend two to four years or even longer on their knowledge products – their research theses. Again, academics and research students may be reluctant to share their research and data for the following two primary reasons: (1) the fear of being criticized for possible errors and weaknesses; (2) the fear of losing the advantages arising from full utilization of the findings and data of their research projects (Hubbard & Little 1997). Southern Cross University's Doctor of Business Administration (DBA) program has implemented some effective pro-knowledge sharing practices to promote knowledge sharing among academics and research students. These include: (1) promoting a knowledge sharing culture and creating an environment for comfortable knowledge sharing; (2) a pod structure for doctoral supervision with a group of candidates and supervisors working together for collaboratively; (3) knowledge management systems, including the online doctoral candidates centre, doctoral supervisors centre, and Elluminate Live (an online communication and learning software); (4) optional colloquia for works-in-progress presentations (5) mandatory doctoral weekend workshops/symposia twice a year; (6) social gatherings for doctoral students and supervisors; (7) a professional development program for supervisors; and (8) a publications program to help researchers publish their work in peer-reviewed conferences and journals (Sankaran, Xu & Sankaran 2007).

An important element for successful knowledge sharing practices is the establishment of a knowledge sharing culture. Changing the existing culture and people's work habits is the main hurdle for most knowledge management programs (McDermott 1999). Previous studies (i.e., Chase 1997; The Conference Board 1999) indicate that the lack of a knowledge sharing culture is the biggest obstacle to knowledge management. The Graduate College of Management (now part of Southern Cross Business School), which runs Southern Cross University's DBA program, has been actively working on creating a pro-knowledge sharing environment (by promoting knowledge sharing in all the public places, including meetings, presentations, workshops, conferences and websites, and establishing and implementing reward programs for good knowledge sharing practices), in which supervisors and candidates feel comfortable and are happy to share their knowledge and discuss their experiences (Sankaran, Xu & Sankaran 2007).

5.5 Summary

Understanding data, information and knowledge is critical to the success of managing knowledge resources in the organization. Several database technologies are available for organisations to manage their data. In the meantime, technologies such as data warehousing and data mining provide organisations with more power to analyse the information they have and thus make better business decisions. But data and data storage come at a cost, especially in the Big Data era; organizations need to effectively use collected information. Meanwhile through systematic knowledge management practices facilitated by knowledge management systems, organizations can better manage their tacit and explicit knowledge. In the next chapter, we will discuss management of information systems infrastructure including hardware, software, networks and telecommunications.

Bibliography

Alavi, M. & Leidner, D.E. 2001, 'Knowledge management and knowledge management systems: Conceptual foundations and research issues', *MIS Quarterly*, Vol. 25, No. 1, pp. 107–146.

Biggs, P., Johnson, T., Lozanova, Y. & Sundberg, N. 2012, 'Emerging issues for our hyper-connected world', in *The Global Information Technology Report 2012: Living in a Hyper-connected World*, Dutta, S. & Bilbao-Osorio, B. eds., INSEAD & World Economic Forum, pp. 47–56.

Bolloju, N., Khalifa, M. & Turban, E. 2002, 'Integrating knowledge management into enterprise environments for the next generation decision support', *Decision Support Systems*, Vol. 33, No. 2, pp. 163–176.

Bonner, D. 2000, *Leading Knowledge Management and Learning*, American Society of Training & Development, Virginia, USA.

Brown, B., Chui, M. & Manika, J. 2011, 'Are you ready for the ear of big data', *McKinsey Quarterly*, October 2011, pp. 1–12.

Bryan, L. L. & Joyce, C. 2005, 'The 21st century organization', *McKinsey Quarterly*, Number 3, 2005, pp. 25–33.

Bughin, J., Livingston, J. & Marwaha, S. 2011, 'Seizing the potential of 'big data'', *McKinsey on Business Technology*, Number 24, Autumn 2011, pp. 8–13.

Chase, R.L. 1997, 'The knowledge-based organization: an international survey', *The Journal of Knowledge Management*, Vol.1, No.1, pp. 38–49.

Chui, M. & Fleming, T. 2011, 'Inside P & G's digital revolution', *McKinsey Quarterly*, November 2011, pp. 1–11.

Conway, R. 2012, 'Where angels will tread', The World in 2012, *The Economist*, January 2012, p. 123.

Davenport, T. H. 2010, 'Rethinking knowledge work: A strategic approach', *McKinsey on Business Technology*, Number 21, Winter 2010, pp. 26–33.

Dijcks, J.P. 2012, 'Big data for the enterprise', *An Oracle White Paper*, January 2012, Oracle Corporation, USA.

Dutta, S., Bilbao-Osorio, B. & Geiger, T. 2012, 'The networked readiness index 2012: Benchmarking ICT progress and impacts for the next decade', in *The Global Information Technology Report 2012: Living in a Hyper-connected World*, Dutta, S. & Bilbao-Osorio, B. eds, INSEAD & World Economic Forum, pp. 3–34.

Haag, S., Baltzan, p. & Phillips, A. 2008, *Business Driven Technology*, 2nd edn, McGraw-Hill Irwin, Boston, USA.

Hagström, M. & Gill, N. 2012, 'The wisdom of the cloud: Hyper-connectivity, big data, and real-time analytics', in *The Global Information Technology Report 2012: Living in a Hyper-connected World*, Dutta, S. & Bilbao-Osorio, B. eds, INSEAD & World Economic Forum, pp. 97–103.

Hubbard, R. & Little, E.L. 1997, 'Share and share alike? A review of empirical Eeidence concerning information sharing among researchers', *Management Research News*, Vol. 20, No. 1, pp. 41–49.

Junnarkar, B. & Brown, C.V. 199), 'Re-Assessing the Enabling Role of Information Technology in KM', *Journal of Knowledge Management*, Vol. 1, No. 2, pp. 142–148.

Laudon, K.C. & Laudon, J.P. 2005, *Essentials of Management Information Systems: Managing the Digital Firm*, 6th edn, Prentice Hall.

Laudon, K.C. & Laudon, J.P. 2012, *Essentials of Management Information Systems: Managing the Digital Firm*, 12th edn, Prentice Hall.

Leonard, D. & Sensiper, S. 1998, 'The role of tacit knowledge in group innovation', *California Management Review*, Vol. 40, No. 3, pp. 112–132.

Lohr, S. 2012, The Age of Big Data, *The New Your Times*, February 11, 2012, Online Available at: http://www.nytimes.com/2012/02/12/sunday-review/big-datas-impact-in-the-world.html?pagewanted=all (accessed August 11, 2012).

Manyika, J. 2009, 'Hal Varian on how the Web challenges managers'', *McKinsey Quarterly*, January 2009, On-line available at: https://www.mckinseyquarterly.com/Strategy/Innovation/Hal_Varian_on_how_the_Web_challenges_managers_2286 (accessed July 23, 2012).

Manyika, J., Chui, M., Brown, B., Bughin, J., Dobbs, R., Roxburgh, C. & Byers, A. H. 2011, *Big Data: The Next Frontier for Innovation, Competition, and Productivity*, McKinsey Global Institute, McKinsey & Company.

McDermott, R. 1999, 'Why information technology inspired but cannot deliver knowledge management', *California Management Review*, Vol. 4, No. 4, pp. 103–117.

Moody, D. L. & Shanks, G.G. 199), 'Using knowledge management and the internet to support evidence based practice: a medical case study', *Proceedings of the 10th Australasian Conference on Information Systems*, Wellington, New Zealand, December 1-3, 1999, pp. 660–676.

Nonaka, I. & Takeuchi, H. 1995, *The Knowledge-Creating Company-How Japanese Companies Create the Dynamic of Innovation*, Oxford University Press, New York.

O'Brien, J. A. & Marakas, G. M. 2011, *Management Information Systems*, 10th Edition, McGraw-Hill, New York, USA.

Oracle 2012, 'Driving innovation through analytics', *Executive Strategy Series*, Oracle Corporation, USA.

Polanyi, M. 1962, *Personal Knowledge: Toward a Post-Critical Philosophy*, Routledge and Kegan Paul, London, UK.

Polanyi, M. 1967, *The Tacit Dimension*, Archor Books, Doubleday, Garden City, New York, USA.

Ruggles, R. 1998, 'The state of the notion: knowledge management in practice', *California Management Review*, Vol. 40, No. 3, pp. 80–89.

SAP AG 2012, 'Harnessing the power of Big Data in real time through in-Memory technology and analytics', in *The Global Information Technology Report 2012: Living in a Hyper-connected World*, Dutta, S. & Bilbao-Osorio, B. eds., INSEAD & World Economic Forum, pp. 89–96.

Shankar, S., Xu, J. & Sankaran, G. 2007, 'Knowledge sharing in doctoral research', *International Technology Management Review*, Vol. 1, No. 1, pp. 34–42.

Siegele L. 2012, 'Welcome to the yotta world', The World in 2012, *The Economist*, January 2012, p. 122.

Spender, J. C. 1996, 'Organizational knowledge, learning, and memory: three concepts in search of a theory', *Journal of Organizational Change Management*, Vol. 9, pp. 63–78.

Stafford, p. 2012, 'How big data can turn the smallest business into Moneyball?', *Smart Company*, Online Available at:http://www.smartcompany.com.au/information-technology/051244-best-of-the-web-how-big-data-can-turn-the-smallest-business-into-moneyball.html?utm_source=SmartCompany&utm_campaign=

8ca827ec42-TechCompany_16_August_201216_08_2012&utm_medium=email (accessed August 16, 2012).

Sveiby, K.E. 1997, *The New Organizational Wealth: Managing and Measuring Knowledge-Based Assets*, Berrett-Koehler Publishers, San Francisco, USA.

The Conference Board 1999, *Beyond Knowledge Management: New Ways to Work and Learn*, The Conference Board Inc, New York, USA.

Chapter 6

Managing Infrastructure for Information Systems

In this chapter, we will provide a managerial view of computer hardware and software; discuss the benefits and opportunities offered by networks and telecommunications; review major types of telecommunications networks; explain how wireless/mobile communication can help an organisation conduct business anytime, anywhere, anyplace; and discuss challenges managers are facing when making decisions on hardware, software, networks, and telecommunications.

6.1 Hardware and Software Management

Computer hardware and software can either improve or impede organisational performance. They are major organisational assets. Therefore it is necessary to properly manage their acquisition and use. Hardware is the equipment, the machinery, the tangible components of information systems. Software is the instructions that tell the hardware what to do. Although managers and business professionals do not need to be experts of hardware and software, a basic understanding of the role of hardware and software will assist them in making good technology decisions thus enhancing business performance and organisational productivity (Laudon & Laudon 2005, p. 192). Some questions on hardware and software in organisations are addressed in the following Table 6.1.

Table 6.1: Some questions on hardware and software

Component	What	Who	Where	How
Hardware	What hardware do we have?	Who manages it?	Where is it located?	How is it used?
			Continued on next page	

Table 6.1 – continued from previous page

Component	What	Who	Where	How
	What computer processing and storage capability does our organization need to handle its information and business transactions	Who uses it?	Where is it used?	How should we acquire and manage the firm's hardware assets?
	What arrangement of computers and computer processing would best benefit our organization?	Who owns it?		How would the new technologies benefit our organization?
	What criteria should we use to select our hardware?			
	What new hardware technologies are available?			
Software	What software do we have?	Who manages it?	Where is it located?	How is it used?
	What new software technologies are available?	Who uses it?	Where is it used?	How should we acquire and manage the firm's software assets?

Continued on next page

Table 6.1 – continued from previous page

Component	What	Who	Where	How
	What kinds of software and software tools do we need to run our business?	Who owns it?		How would the new software technologies benefit our organization?
	What criteria should we use to select our software technology?			
	What new software technologies are available?			

(Sources: Developed from Pearlson & Saunders 2004, p. 134; Pearlson & Saunders 2010, p. 169; Laudon & Laudon 2005, pp. 225–226)

6.1.1 Trends of hardware and software

The trend of hardware is towards easy to use, maintain, and connect via telecommunications links through organisations (i.e. the shift from central computing via main frame computer to networked computing in the format of peer-to-peer, client-server and grid computing). The trend of software development is towards easy to use and multipurpose network-enabled application packages for productivity and collaboration. One particular trend is demands such as "the Internet in the pocket", "the Internet on the move", "personal computer in the pocket", and "personal computer on the move". Device manufacturers and software developers need to address such demands by working on devices (especially tablets, smart phones) and applications for mobility. Bisson, Stephenson and Patrick Viguerie (2010) suggest that the percentages of mobile phone users have jumped from 3% of the world population 15% years ago to 50%; nearly 50% of all new mobile phones purchased in developed markets are now Internet-ready smartphones; and within just three years of IPhone's launch developers have done more than 200,000 applications.

IDG Connect (2012) finds out that a majority (71%) of business and information systems executives around the world own tablets.

6.1.2 *Evaluation of hardware and software*

How do companies evaluate and select hardware and software? When making decisions on hardware, there is much more to evaluating hardware than deciding the fastest and cheapest computer devices. Some specific questions have to be asked and evaluated (O'Brien & Marakas 2006, p. 420):

- Performance: speed, capacity, and throughput.
- Cost: lease or purchase price, cost of operations and maintenance, total cost of ownership.
- Reliability: risk of malfunction & maintenance requirements, error control and diagnostic features.
- Compatibility: with existing hardware and software? with hardware & software provided by competing suppliers?
- Connectivity: easily connected to WANs and LANs that use different types of network technologies and bandwidth alternatives?
- Scalability: can it handle the processing demands of end users, transactions, queries, & other processing requirements?
- Software: is system and application software available that can best use this hardware?
- Support: is support available?
- Ergonomics: user-friendly? safe, comfortable, and easy to use? human factors engineered?
- Technology: year of product life cycle? does it use a new, untested technology? does it run the risk of obsolescence?

Many factors for software evaluation would be the same as those used for hardware evaluation since software and hardware are intertwined (i.e. without software hardware can do nothing while without hardware software is useless) (O'Brien & Marakas 2006, p. 421). However there are also some additional factors specially designed for software evaluation:

- Quality: bug free?
- Efficiency: well-developed system of program code that does not use much CPU time, memory capacity, or disk space?
- Flexibility: Can it handle our processes easily without major modification?

- Security: Does it provide control procedures for errors, malfunctions, and improper use?
- Connectivity: Web-enabled?
- Language: Is the programming language familiar to internal software developers?
- Documentation: well-documented? Help screens and helpful software agents?
- Hardware: Does existing hardware have the features required to best use this software?
- Other factors: Performance, cost (total cost of ownership), reliability, availability, usefulness, ease of use, compatibility, modularity, technology, ergonomics, scalability, and support characteristics.

Many vendors of hardware and software and other firms offer a variety of information systems services to end users and organisations, i.e. assisting in developing a web site, data migration from old/legacy systems to new systems, installing or converting of new hardware and software, employee training, and hardware maintenance (O'Brien & Marakas 2006, p. 422). Sometimes, some of these services are provided by the vendors free. Other kinds of services can be outsourced to an outside company for certain fees. Evaluation factors of information systems services focusing on the quality of support services include:

- Performance: record of past performance?
- Systems development: Are website and other e-business developers available? What are their quality and cost?
- Maintenance: Is equipment maintenance provided? What are its quality and cost?.
- Conversion: What systems development and installation services will they provide during the conversion period?
- Training: Is the necessary training of personnel provided? What are its quality and cost?
- Backup: Are similar computer facilities available nearby for emergency backup purposes?
- Accessibility: Dose the vendor provide local or regional sites that offer sales, systems development, and hardware maintenance services? Is a customer support center at the vendor's website available? Is a customer hot line provided?
- Business position: Is the vendor financially strong, with good industry market prospects?
- Hardware: Do they provide a wide selection of compatible hardware devices and accessories?
- Software: Do they offer a variety of useful e-business software and application packages?

By surveying 3,124 global IT and business professionals, IDG Connect (2012) identifies five factors important for owners and potential owners of tablets, including functionality, applications availability, branding, appearance and price.

6.2 Networks and Telecommunications Management

Telecommunications and network technologies are connecting and revolutionising business and society. We are now live in a world of "The Global Grid": everyone and everything is connected (Bisson, Stephenson and Patrick Viguerie (2010). Many organisations today could not survive without a variety of interconnected computer networks to service their information processing and communications needs. Businesses have become networked enterprises, where the Internet, intranets and extranets are networking to business processes and employees and linking them to their customers, suppliers and other business stakeholders (O'Brien & Marakas 2011, p. 218).

A computer network consists of a group of two or more computer systems linked together using wires, radio waves or other communication media over a geographical area (Haag, Baltzan & Phillips 2006, p. 384). Wireless communication is one of the fastest growing areas (Haag, Baltzan & Phillips 2006, p. 384). Networks enable the enterprise to collaborate more creatively with its employees and its customers, suppliers, and other stakeholders, manage the business operations and organisational resources more effectively, and compete successfully in today's fast changing global economy (O'Brien & Marakas 2011, p. 278). Telecommunications is 'the exchange of information in any form (voice, data, text, images, audio, and video) over networks' (O'Brien & Marakas 2011, p. 278). While knowledge of technical details may not be that important for managers, a good understanding of the concepts and basic terminology is. Managers should be particularly aware of the business values and opportunities provided to businesses through networks and telecommunications.

6.2.1 *Business values and trends of telecommunications*

Telecommunications can help companies overcome barriers to business success. O'Brien and Marakas (2011, p. 224) suggest that telecommunications have four strategic capabilities: (1) overcoming geographic barriers (i.e., capturing information in real time from various locations); (2) overcoming time barriers (i.e., providing in-time services to different regions); (3) overcoming cost barriers (i.e., reducing the costs of communications by fewer travels); and (4) overcoming structural barriers (i.e., utilizing the Internet, intranets and extranets to link with customers, suppliers, partners and strategic alliances).

In the meantime, major trends occurring in the field of telecommunications have a significant impact on management decisions in this area. Managers should thus be aware of major trends in telecommunications industries (i.e., moving toward more competitive market and more collaboration and co-opetition among device manufacturers, software makers, telecommunication carriers, network services providers), technologies (i.e., moving toward more use of Internet technologies and networks for better and faster multimedia communications), and applications (towards more to development of collaborative applications by taking advantages of the availability of networks and large scale adoption of cheaper and faster mobile devices across the globe) that significantly increase the decision alternatives confronting their organisations (O'Brien & Marakas 2011, p. 221). At the same time, as Eric Schmidt, Google's Chairman and former CEO aruges (reported in Manyika 2008) argues, in the digital world and the networked economy, the cost of transmission and distribution of information has becoming lower and lower even though it is still very costly to build underlying infrastructure (in fact it is a long term investment. The Internet we have today is largely a result of the investments made about 20 years ago during the first wave of Internet booming).

Currently a consortium of more than 300 universities, government agencies and private businesses that are collaborating to find ways to make the Internet more efficient is working on the project of the next generation of Internet – Internet2 (http://www.internet2.edu). The primary goals of the Internet2 project are: creating a leading edge very-high speed network for the research community, enabling revolutionary Internet applications, and ensuring the rapid transfer of new network services and applications to the broader Internet community. Internet2 is a high-performance network that uses an entirely different infrastructure than the public Internet we know today. But Internet2 was never intended to replace the Internet, rather its purpose is to build a road map that can be followed when the next stage of innovation to the current Internet takes place. Most institutions and commercial partners are connected via Abilene, a network backbone that will soon support throughput of 10 gigabits per second. Internet2 is all about high-speed telecommunications and infinite bandwidth. What do you think the Internet will 'look' like in 10-years time? On a related note, while IPV4 has around 4 billion (2^{32} IP addresses), IPV6 (2^{128} IP addresses) could allocate each human being on the earth a few IP addresses (Biggs *et al.* 2012, p. 52).

6.2.2 The Internet of Things

The Internet of Things refer to objects embedded with sensors and actuators and linked with wired and wireless network (Chui, Löffle & Roberts 2010). They have the ability to sense the environment and deliver large volume of data through networks-in fact machines such as The Internet of things generally much more data than human beings. According to Bisson, Stephenson and Patrick Viguerie (2010), there are more than 35 billion of Internet Things (including sensors, routers, cameras, and the like). And the number is growing very quickly.

The Internet of Things could assist organizations' efforts of Information & Analysis and Automation & Control (Chui, Löffler & Roberts 2010):

- Tracking behaviour: monitoring the behaviour of persons, things, or data through space and time (i.e., targeted advertising based on the location of the users of smart phones; real-time information of movement of packages from warehouse to end user).
- Enhanced situational awareness: realizing real-time and accurate information of physical environment (i.e., utilizing sensor networks that combine video, audio and vibration detectors to identify unauthorized individuals and crime suspects).
- Supporting decision making via sensor-driven business analytics: supporting long-range and more complex planning and decision making (i.e., remote monitoring and controlling oil & gas operations; remote monitoring and controlling medical procedures).
- Optimizing resource consumption and management: monitoring and controlling resource consumption across network (i.e., managing consumption (and pricing) of water, electricity and energy via networked sensors and automatic feedback mechanism).
- Improving processes: automation of processes by having much better information granularity (i.e., automation of chemical plants by utilizing sensors and actuators along the production lines).
- Enhanced ability (especially in open environments with great uncertainty): rapid and real-time sensing and responding systems (i.e., sensors in the two cars could detect and avoid potential collision between them).

6.2.3 Types of telecommunications networks

Major types of telecommunications networks, which serve as the telecommunication infrastructure for the Internet and networked enterprises, consist of: Wide Area Network (WAN), Local Area Networks (LAN), Metropolitan area network (MAN), Virtual Private Network

(VPN), Client/Server Network and Peer-to-Peer (P2P) Network (O'Brien & Marakas 2011, p. 238; Haag, Baltzan & Phillips 2006, pp. 386, 396; Laudon & Laudon 2012, p. 281).

Haag, Baltzan and Phillips (2006, p. 386) point out that Wide Area Networks (WAN) cover a large geographic area while Local Area Networks (LAN) connect computers & other information processing devices within a limited physical area. Metropolitan area network (MAN) spans a metropolitan area, usually a city and its major suburbs. Its geographic scope falls between WAN and LAN. A Virtual Private Network (VPN) provides a secure connection between two points across a public network (i.e., the Internet) to transmit data and provides a low-cost alternative to a private network (O'Brien & Marakas 2011, p. 239).

A client/server network is designed to combine the best features of mainframes and personal computers. The clients share processing tasks in a network that is connected to a host computer called a server, which provides files, responds to database queries or handles high-speed processing. In most cases, it controls access to the network, manages communication between personal computers and makes data & program files available to the clients. In client/server environment, computing processing is split between client machines and server machines linked to a network. End users interface with the client machines (Laudon & Laudon 2005, pp. 201–202).

A client/server network distributes much of the organisation's computing power to the desktop and factory floor (Laudon & Laudon 2005, p. 268). The Internet is based on client/server technology. End users using the Internet control their activities through client applications, such as web browsers. All the data, including email messages and web pages, are stored on servers. A client uses the Internet to request information from a particular remote web server and the server sends back the information via Internet. With Peer-to-peer (P2P) networks computers can function as both servers and workstations (Haag, Baltzan & Phillips 2006, p. 394). A Grid computing network is one form of P2P network which applies computational resources of many networked computers to solve large, complex problems (Laudon & Laudon 2005, p. 203).

6.3 Wireless Communication

Mobile (or wireless) devices (such as laptops, tablet-computers, smart phones and other mobile devices) can connect to the Internet via wireless points which link to the Internet via land-based and wired connections (Laudon & Traver 2012, p. 306). Wireless technologies are transforming how we live, work, and play. Wireless devices provide users with a live

(Internet) connection via satellite or radio transmitters. Wireless telecommunications technologies rely on radio wave, microwave, infrared, and visible light pulses to transport digital communications without wires between communications devices (O'Brien & Marakas 2006, p. 194). Through adopting wireless technologies organisations can establish a live connection for their employees, customers, and suppliers to access their organisational information and applications anytime, anywhere, and anyplace. Handheld devices are increasingly offering additional functionality and cellular networks are advancing rapidly in their increased speed and throughput abilities (O'Brien & Marakas 2006, p. 196). These enabling technologies are fuelling the widespread adoption and creation of new and innovative ways to perform business. A contemporary corporate telecommunications system is a collection of many different networks (i.e., wired LAN, mobile Wi-Fi network, wireless LAN, Intranet, Extranet, Internet, Telephone system) via both wired and wireless communication media (i.e., websites, mobile devices, PCs, laptops, servers) (Laudon & Laudon 2012, p. 277).

6.4 Management challenges

6.4.1 *Understanding Global ICT Industry*

According to a recent study by the consulting firm Booz & Company on Global ICT (information and communication technology) companies reported in Acker, Gröne and Schröder (2012), top ten ICT leaders are (in the order): Mircrosoft, Oracle, IBM, HP, Cisco Systems, Apple, SAP, Xerox, Accenture and CSC. The ranking is completed by looking at each firm's performance in the perspectives of: financial performance (i.e., how is the ability of sustaining the profitability needed to make future investments), portfolio strength (i.e., how good is the mix of different products/services), go-to-market footprint (i.e., how is the sales and delivery capabilities in the top markets for ICT), and growth potential (i.e., how is innovation capacity? presence in the emerging markets? the ability to attract new customers?).

In addition, in the above-mentioned study by Booz & Company reported in Acker, Gröne and Schröder (2012), they have grouped top 50 ICT firms into four categories:
- Hardware and infrastructure firms: including HP, Apple, Samsung, Dell, Fujitsu, Cisco Systems, NEC, Ericsson, Xerox, and Alcatel Lucent
- Software and Internet firms: including Microsoft, Oracle, Google, SAP, Yahoo, SAP, Yahoo, Symantec, Intuit, Adobe, Amdocs, and Convergys

- Information syetems service providers (Global firms, regional providers, and offshore firms in emerging markets): including IBM, Accenture, CSC, Capgemini, First Data, Tata Consulting Services, Hitachi, Wipro, Atos, Infosys, Logica, Cognozant, Capita, Unisys, IT Holdings, HCL, Indra, Steria, and Tieto
- Telecom operating firms (mobile, landline, Internet and television): including NTT, AT & T, Verizon, Deutsche Telecom, Telefonica, Vodafone, France Telecom, KDDI, British Telecom, and KPN.

Meanwhile the emerging trends in the ICT industry are:

- Hardware and infrastructure firms such as Apple, HP, Dell, Cisco Systems and Xerox while they are still focusing on their core business (i.e., building more powerful and affordable devices and equipment), they are also working hard on differentiation strategy and branching out into Software and Service areas.
- Software and Internet firms are expanding into other areas selectively. Large firms are either entering certain new territories (i.e., Yahoo offering comprehensive web hosting services, Microsoft and Google embarking on hardware business) or focusing on enhancing their lead in the industry (i.e., via acquisition and consolidation-an example is Oracle's move to the complete integration skills through acquisition of Sun Microsystems to seek for markets traditionally owned by system integrators and information systems service providers). Other smaller players are trying to be specialized and sufficiently distinctive and create relatively protected platforms for growth.
- Global information systems service providers such as IBM and CSC are starting offering some telecom services (i.e., telephony services by IBM and conferencing solutions by CSC) while they are keeping their large scale and industry leading position. Regional service providers (i.e., Atos in France, Logica in the UK, and Unisys in the US) are working on expanding their market share and increase their scale (i.e., through mergers and acquisitions) while offshore firms (especially firms in India such as HCL, Infosys and Wipro) are actively entering ICT developed markets (including the U.S., the U. K., Japan, Germany, France-these five markets contributed 60% of Global ICT sales in 2011) by leveraging advantages of large pool of talent with lower salaries. In addition, the "follow-the-sun" delivery (i.e., a project could be worked on from different locations in different zones 24 hours a day) become a reality as a result of global connectedness.
- Although Telecom firms have not been active in investing in innovating as a result of the on-going investments required for network structure and dividend commitments, they are

starting cross boundaries and entering into information systems service areas (i.e., Verison and NTT's offerings for cloud computing services).
- Integration is an important information systems service area for ICT firms for reasons such as the wide adoption of cloud-based applications and the ever increasing demand for enterprise mobility. ICT firms working in or intending to embark on service areas should upgrade or complete their integration skills
- For most ICT firms their main revenue are still coming from classic ICT products and services, and the financial performance of new (or so called next generation) products and services (i.e., highly specialized services, RFID solutions, near-field communications, cloud computing, mobile computing, and social computing) will be realized in the future.
- As ICT firms compete across boundaries, the winners are those firms that are more innovative, more responsive to customers, and better able to deliver more with lower costs. In order to stay ahead of the competition, they have to be fast-moving, flexible and with something distinctive that no other firms can duplicate/copy.
- ICT firms also need to be aware non-ICT firms could be major competitors and venture into areas of ICT firms, for example Amazon is providing many products and services traditionally covered by ICT firms.

Another emerging trend is the fight for standards (including standards in operation systems) and patents in the ICT industry even though it could be common to other industries. Apple's iOS versus Google's Android operation systems in the smart domain and Apple vesus Samsung in patents of mobile phone design and features just two interesting cases among many others (to come!).

6.4.2 *Some questions needed to be asked about information systems infrastructure*

Information systems infrastructure is fundamental to the effective deliveries of required information systems capabilities for the business and critical to the organizational performance (especially in today's networked/digital economy). To successfully manage information systems infrastructure, organizations need to look at their management practices and ask themselves a few question in this regard (Kaplan 2011; Markus 2012; The Authors Own Knowledge):
- How to effectively manage the increasing demand and the cost for better infrastructure?: While business leaders are demanding better technology capacity to support business/revenue growth, organizations need to make informed decision by effectively manag-

ing demand (i.e., via prioritizing the demand as per strategic objectives and goals of the business) and taking advantages of emerging/new technologies (i.e., technologies for social, mobile and location computing as well as cloud-computing and global connectedness).

- What is the contingency plan for the current economic situation or even worse one?: Organizations need to look at how they work on their information systems investments in the unstable economic situation and should be ready for scenarios such as how can we get required IS/IT capabilities and stay with the competition with reduced budget (10%? 20%? 30%?....)?
- Which and how much infrastructure capability will be needed in the near term?, medium term?, and long term?: Organizations need to have short, media and long term plans to survive, grow and prosper.
- What is required infrastructure for our globalization efforts?: A global infrastructure strategy needs to be properly planned and executed by taking into consideration of political, technological, economic and social (including cultural elements) factors of different markets (especially those large emerging markets)
- What are our approach in dealing with the capabilities of new technologies and associated risks?: New and emerging technologies such as cloud computing applications could be bring benefits (including lower costs and increased agility) to organizations (especially to small and medium enterprises while concerns and risks such as availability, privacy, security could be brought serious damage/harm to the business.) However, organizations should not stay away from new technologies just because they are not 100% risk free. In fact, organizations should actively look at leveraging the advantages and opportunities arising from new technologies with a well-thought plan and process (i.e., looking at perspectives of adopting new technologies such as demand, value, architecture, organization & governance, and vendor selection), while having an effective risk management strategy in place (and allocating sufficient resources for it).
- What is you're approach and process to manage IS/IT investments?: Organizations need to have an effective process for selecting and measuring IS/IT investments and should have an IS/IT investment committee or steering committee, which involves relevant stakeholders from business and IT areas.
- Have we managed good relations with regulators and relevant agencies?: To some extent (less for some industries and more (even much more) for other industries, organizations' IS/IT infrastructure investments are a result of regulatory requirements. Having good relations with regulators and relevant agencies will definitely make the job of complying with

regulations easier, reduce the cost of doing it, and put organizations in better position for anticipating and preparing for the expected/informed changes!.

6.4.3 *Centralisation or decentralisation*

Centralised computing can give organisations benefits such as: more control since all processing is accomplished by one large central computer (i.e. mainframe computer), consistent standards & common data, economies of scale & shared services, accss to large capacity, better recruitment and training of information systems professionals, and better bargaining power when negotiating with suppliers, but may lead to such issues as not meeting local needs, slow support for strategic initiatives, tension between business and information systems function, and lack of business unit control over overhead costs (Pearlson & Saunders 2010, p. 233; O'Brien & Marakas 2006, p. 481, Laudon & Laudon 2005, p. 192).

On the other hand, distributed computing, such as client/server, peer to peer (P2P), and grid computing, distributes computing powers among computers in different locations/functions. It gives such benefits as more power for local operations, departments, divisions and end users, looking after local needs, closer partnership between business and information system, better flexibility, and better cost control; but it can lead to issues such as lack of consistency of standards, loss of control, duplication of staff & data, difficulty in getting preferred contracts/agreements, and higher costs (Pearlson & Saunders 2010, p. 233; O'Brien & Marakas 2006, p. 481; Laudon & Laudon 2005, p. 192). So what is the best? How much to centralise or distribute? Answers vary for different needs of various organisations. Organisations should choose the computing model compatible with organisational goals. They also should assess the costs and benefits. For example, networked computers and centralised computing could increase management's control, but what happens if there is a failure in network? (Laudon & Laudon 2005, p. 192).

6.4.4 *Selecting appropriate technologies for enterprise networking*

Internet technologies (i.e. different networks and network services, XML and Java) have dramatically enhanced organisations' capacity for connectivity and integration of various applications. However, there is still a lot to do. Many companies are facing the challenge of integrating and coordinating various applications and systems (Laudon & Laudon 2005, p. 266).

There are different standards for linkage with different networks. Networks operated on one standard may not be able to link to those networks based on other standards. Addressing this problem leads to investment on additional equipment and management overheads. Furthermore, integration of business applications from different vendors may require integration software (i.e. middleware) that can support the firm's business processes and data structures. Open standard for interoperability of applications from different vendors is a way to go. For example, Open Mobile Alliance (OMA) (http://www.openmobilealliance.org/), which includes more than 300 companies representing mobile operators, device and network suppliers, information technology companies, and content providers, has actively pursued the Open Standard for interoperability of various mobile data services from different vendors across devices, geographies, service providers, operators, and networks.

Networks and telecommunications technologies that meet today's requirements may lack the connectivity for domestic or global expansion in the future (Laudon & Laudon 2005, p. 266). Strategic telecommunications planning, which can be a part of a firm's strategic information systems planning, can ensure the firm's telecommunications and networks address the business needs, respond to the market changes, and plan for the connectivity and application integration needed (Laudon & Laudon 2005, p. 287). For example, wireless (mobile) technologies promise to be the next major development in e-commerce both for business and consumer markets (B2B and B2C). Businesses should closely examine how wireless technologies can support their operations, enhance their business performance, and generate new opportunities through mobile business/mobile commerce. Organisations also should take a broader perspective on infrastructure development and can no longer develop and implement telecommunications networks confined to organisational boundaries. The new information systems infrastructure for a networked enterprise should connect the whole enterprise and link it with other organisations and the public. Balancing network reliability and availability against mushrooming network costs also needs to be considered (Laudon & Laudon 2005, p. 266). On the one hand, networking is the foundation of digital economy/society; on the other hand although telecommunications transition costs are decreasing, total network capacity (bandwidth) requirements (are growing very fast, which will lead to massive increases in costs to business (Laudon & Laudon 2005, p. 266).

Another very important role of telecommunications & networks planning is to help managers with decisions about selecting telecommunications technologies and services to enhance the performance of the firm. Laudon and Laudon (2005, p. 288; 2012, pp. 224-

225) suggest some factors to consider when a business is embarking on new telecommunications technologies. These factors include:
- Distance: Are future telecommunication needs primarily local or long distance?
- Services: range of functions and services needed? (email? electronic data interchange? wireless? voice mail? videoconferencing? graphics & multimedia transition? need of integration of different services?).
- Point of access: number of locations needed for services and capabilities?
- Utilisation: anticipated frequency and volume of communications?
- Security and reliability of the proposed new telecommunications systems
- Scalability of the proposed new telecommunications systems: not only for current demand but also for future demand.
- Connectivity: How easy or difficult (i.e. required time, money and effort) is it to connect disparate components of network or networks?
- Flexibility/adaptability: Can the proposed telecommunications applications be adapted to the changes in the market place?
- Purchasing & maintaining its own Or renting from external suppliers? What are benefits? risks? benefits versus risks?
- Cost: What is the cost of proposed telecommunication technology?, What are some variable costs?, How about fixed cost?, Any hidden cost?, direct and indirect costs?, and what is total cost of ownership (hardware, software account for only about 20% of total cost of ownership! Other costs include: installation, training, support, maintenance, infrastructure, downtime, space and energy. Total cost of ownership can be reduced through the adoption of cloud services, greater centralization, and standardization of hardware and software resources).

On a related note, some typical components of total cost of ownership include (Laudon & Laudon 2012, p. 226):
- Hardware acquisition: purchase price or lease costs of computer hardware equipment including computers, terminals, storage, and printers.
- Software acquisition: purchase price or license fees of software for each user.
- Installation: cost to install computers and software (large organizations normally do this themselves via their information systems operation/function).
- Training: cost to provide training for information systems specialists and end users
- Support: cost to provide on-going technical support, help desks and so forth.

- Infrastructure: cost to acquire, maintain, and support related infrastructure, such as networks and specialized equipment (including storage backup units).
- Downtime: cost of lost productivity if hardware and software failures cause the system to be unavailable for processing and user tasks.
- Space and Energy: real estate and utility costs for housing and providing power for the technology (i.e., data centers for large organizations).

6.4.5 *The emergence of web computing*

Google along with others are moving computing to the web and away from the desktop. To use web-based applications, we require: a computer, the Internet connection, and an Internet browser (i.e. Microsoft's Internet Explorer, Mozilla's Firefox). And they are independent of operating systems (i.e. Windows operating systems) in the same way desktop applications are. While personal computers allow you to perform tasks which could previously only be done by a mainframe, the Internet allow you to self-selected applications and put them together for your use. Web computing provides you an operating environment but not an operating system, and it moves from client/server to client/web. With a web-based platform, information systems will be easier, faster and cheaper to use. For example, you don't need to install/download anything for using various Google services/applications except an Internet browser.

6.4.6 *Web services, SOA, grid computing, cloud computing, virtualisation*

Web services and service oriented architecture (SOA), grid computing, cloud computing, and virtualisation , can enable businesses to (1) have better inter-operability and integration of their various applications from different vendors in different languages, formats, platforms, (2) better utilise and streamline their information systems resources, (3) look at delivering computing as a service rather than a product; and (4) thus improve the efficiency and effectiveness of their information systems investments.

However the adoption and diffusion of these technologies, methodologies, and approaches are still in the early stage. A lot has to be done (i.e., standards and standardization, open interface, network reliability & 24/7/365 availability everywhere for everyone).

6.4.7 Cloud Computing

Cloud computing basically is renting computing resources (including software, networks, servers, storage, processing, operation systems, applications, services) on the networks (especially the Internet) as per usage, and it can deploy in the models of private cloud (solely for one firm and could be managed by the organization or a third party on its premise or off its premise), public cloud (is made to the general public or a large industry group and is owned by an organization selling cloud services), and hybrid cloud (the combination of private and public) (Compuware 2010; Trend Micro 2010). By adopting cloud-computing, organizations could (1) better utilize there IS/IT investments; (2) have better flexibility, quicker responses to changes, enhanced ability for information systems to scale up, better ability of disaster recovery and business continuity; and (3) focus on their core business (especially for small and medium firms). One good example (reported in Roberts, Sarrazin & Sikes 2010) is by using Amazon.com's cloud computing facilities, The New York Times digitalized and catalogued more than 100 years of archived articles for its web in a 24-hour period, avoiding the need to configure and run a set of servers for a onetime effort. In line with the rapid progress and huge potential of Cloud computing, major ICT firms have committed significant resources to cloud computing developments.

Some typical technologies associated with cloud computing include virtualization and service-oriented architecture. It could be argued that the approach of clouding computing is not really new (i.e., thinking about the example of mainframe computer to individual users of it). The difference is between sharing computing resources on the networks (there are more than 50 million servers and most of them operates only at 15% of capacity (Intel Corporation 2011; Harvard Business Review 2010)) and sharing the main-frame computer. Some characteristics of cloud computing consist of: (1) on-demand self-service (for example, required computing resources could be run automatically without human interaction once the parameter and instruction are set); (2) broad network access (can be accessed by various devices such as mobile devices, personal computers, laptops); (3) resource pooling (the provider's computing resources are pooled to serve multiple clients simultaneously by using a multi-tenant model); (4) rapid elasticity (the ability of quickly scaling out and scaling in according to the changes in demand); and (5) measured service (adopting metering capability for transparency in monitoring, controlling and reporting) (Compuware Corporation 2010).

Cloud service models include (Trend Micro 2010: Intel Corporation 2011; Compuware Corporation 2010):

- Cloud Software as a Service (SaaS): providing customer with the capability to use the provider's applications sitting on a cloud infrastructure. Examples of SaaS include Google's Gmail system and Microsoft's Office 365.
- Cloud Platform as a Service (PaaS): providing customer with the capability to deploy applications on the cloud platform using programming languages and tools supported by the cloud provider, who has full control of the cloud infrastructure. Examples include Microsoft's Windows Azure and Google App engine.
- Closed Infrastructure as a Service (IaaS): the consumer has the ability to access processing, storage, networks and other fundamental computing resources and run arbitrary software such as operating systems and applications. But such computing resources controlled by the customer are typically for securing their own virtual machines and applications & data residing on them, the cloud provider still controls the underlying cloud infrastructure. Examples include Amazon EC2 and vCloud.

Meanwhile some top concerns of cloud computing are: security, privacy, and availability & performance (Trend Micro 2010; Compuware 2010, Intel Corporation 2011). Security and privacy issues are very critical and typical for cloud computing since you have put your critical information/data in other people's properties and you have no good idea and have no effective control regarding what is going to happen to your data/information. Furthermore issues such as multi-tenancy (you are completely unaware of your neighbour's identity, security profile or intention), data access control and protection (the cloud provider could easily move around your data for their purposes), and data romance (there is no clear standard on how the cloud provider should recycle memory and disk space). So it is likely the next user of your ex-rented cloud computing resources could have your critical and confidential data), and data privacy issues (for example, data losses/leakage and breaches are top security concerns of cloud computing, especially for public cloud) further highlight the need for effective security management of information/data in the cloud.

Organizations need to put in place effective security management process and tools (i.e., encryption, good security/encryption key management access control, auditing) to protect the information in the cloud. Availability & performance issues are logic concerns when you are relying on other people's services. At the moment, even you host applications/systems in your organization, the availability is around 99% since the networks are controlled by the telecoms, and while you put your applications/systems with the cloud service provider, the availability may become $99\% \times 99\% \times 99\%...$ since problems may come from each part of the cloud chain. One effective way to deal with such issues are to sign a service level agreement (SLA) with cloud service provider. Another concern is the hidden costs in the cloud, and organizations need to pay close to attention to data transfer charges, which could increase dramatically once required cloud service and computing power grow to a certain level (Harvard Business Review 2010). Some other concerns include the need for adapting business processes to cloud applications, addressing issues with integration and interoperability with the firm's computing infrastructure, adjusting technology governance processes (i.e., policies for control, monitoring) for cloud applications, and developing the required skills for managing cloud applications (Roberts & Sikes 2011).

6.4.8 *Mobile Computing*

El-Darwiche, Singh & Genediwalla (2012) suggest that more people today have access to a mobile phone than to electricity. Bold and Davidson (2012, p. 71) suggest that the installed base of smartphones exceeded that of PCs in 2011 and is growing more than three times faster than personal computers, and the expected shipment of smartphones between 2011 and 2015 could be around 4 billion. Today's smartphones deliver increasing rich experiences to consumers, including full web-browsing and computing capabilities, high-definition video, 3D gaming, access to social networks, and many other compelling services. Garner reported in May 2011 (cited in Bold & Davidson 2012, p. 72) that total download of mobile applications reached 8 billion in 2010 and should surpass 100 billion by 2015. Ericsson estimates (cited in Dutta, Bilbao-Osorio & Geiger (2012, p. 3)) there will be more than 50 billion connected devices in the world by 2020. It is reported (cited in Berman & Bell 2011) by the end of 2011, smart phones and tablet-computers will overtake personal computer shipments; and downloads of mobile applications (Apps) are expected to surge from 11 billion in 2010 to 77 billion in 2014.

Mobility is becoming an important agenda for organizations as a result of the wide adoption of mobile devices (especially smart phones and tablets), the availability of fast cabled and wireless networks (i.e., 3G, 4G), and the explosion of innovative mobile applications. According to a recent McKinsey survey of 250 CIOs on their organizations' mobile strategies (cited in Akella *et al.* 2012), 56% of respondents reported demand from employees to support a wide range of mobile devices, 77% were going to allow staff to use personal mobile devices to access company data and applications, and nearly 100% expected to deploy more than 25 mobile applications in the next two years. The survey also identified top three challenges for mobile computing: (1) security concerns (wireless communication is more vulnerable than wired one, and the mobile devices have higher chance of getting lost or stolen because of their smaller size); (2) costs (including costs for devices, connectivity, applications, maintenance & support); and (3) associated organizational challenges (i.e., fit with existing structure, process, information systems development & management, infrastructure, and governance required for mobile computing). In line with the results of the survey, Akella *et al.* (2012) suggest four steps for implementing a holistic mobility strategy: (1) defining your mobile policy, (2) developing the support/required infrastructure for mobile computing, (3) identifying priority user segments and meeting their needs (i.e., field people and sales/marketing people will be the major users for whom extensive access to firms' data and applications should be provided while for others access to email, calendar and other simple applications or long-tail applications could be provided), and (4) integrating mobility into computing capabilities of the organization (and making mobile computing a part of information systems governance).

6.4.9 *Integration*

When organizations are embarking on exciting opportunities and capabilities offered by various technologies and leveraging advantages from multiple channels (i.e., call centers, stores/branches, online operations, mobile applications, videos, fax machines, agents and third parties), one critical factor is integration. They need to appropriately integrate various applications/systems with their information systems infrastructure or/and existing applications/systems and unify different channels to share information across the organization. Technologies such as service-oriented architecture, which can create a unified business-service layer for channels and front-end processes to share (customer) information, could be useful in this regard and help win or retain customers. For example, if a customer called before walking into a store, if such information is not managed and shared across the organization and the multiple channels, then the opportunity of wining the customer could be gone (Wang 2010). One particular relevant point at the moment is to integrate mobile devices (such as smart phones, tablets) into the IS/IT infrastructure so the owners of those mobile devices could securely and smoothly access the required information and use corporate applications from them (mobile devices) (Kleiner 2012).

The next generation of the Internet standards such as HTLM5 will provide the access to all programs and applications via a web browser from any device anywhere anytime. HTML5 arguably is the most significant evolution yet in web standards, and it could locally store 1,000 times more data in browsers than they currently do (Korkmaz, Lee & Park 2011).

It allows programs/applications to run through web browsers and communicate different multimedia content without requiring plug-in software and other workarounds.

6.5 Summary

An information system is composed of hardware, software, people, data, and telecommunications networks. Hardware is a vital part of computer systems and provides the underlying physical foundation for firms' information systems infrastructure. Other infrastructure components of software, data and networks require hardware for their storage and operation. To be useful, hardware needs software, which gives instructions that control the operation of a computer system. Networks enable large and small businesses to communicate internally between staff and externally with suppliers, customers, government and the marketplace. Networks are fundamental to online businesses and digital enterprises. Making the right decision in relation to information systems infrastructure is vital to the success of the business. In the next chapter, we will discuss the need for cross-functional information systems and look at how organizations can use enterprise resource planning systems for improving internal operational efficiency.

Bibliography

Acker, O., Gröne, F. & Schröder, G. 2012, 'The Global ICT 50: the supply side of digitization', *Strategy + Business*, July 2012, pp. 1–9.

Akella, J., Brown, B., Gilbert, G., & Wong, L. 2012, 'Mobility disruption: A CIO perspective', *Business Technology Office, McKinsey & Company*, September 2012, Online Available at: https://www.mckinseyquarterly.com/Business_Technology/BT_Strategy/Mobility_disruption_A_CIO_perspective_3019 (accessed Sep 20, 2012).

Biggs, p., Johnson, T., Lozanova, Y. & Sundberg, N. 2012, 'Emerging issues for our hyper-connected world', in *The Global Information Technology Report 2012: Living in a Hyper-connected World*, Dutta, S. & Bilbao-Osorio, B. eds, INSEAD & World Economic Forum, pp. 47–56.

Bisson, p., Stephenson, E. & Patrick Viguerie, S. 2010, 'The global grid', *McKinsey Quarterly*, June 2010, pp. 1–7.

Bold, W. & Davidson, W. 2012, 'Mobile Broadband: Redefining Internet access and empowering individuals', in *The Global Information Technology Report 2012: Living in a Hyper-connected World*, Dutta, S. & Bilbao-Osorio, B. eds., INSEAD & World Economic Forum, pp. 67–77.

Chui, M. Löffler, M. & Roberts, R. 2010, 'The Internet of Things', *McKinsey Quarterly*, Number 2 2010, pp. 1–9.

Compuware Corporation 2010, 'Performance in the Cloud', *White Paper: Cloud Computing 2010*, Corpuware Corporation USA, pp. 1–6.

Haag, S., Baltzan, p. & Phillips, A. 2006, *Business Driven Technology*, 1st edition, McGraw-Hill Irwin, Boston, USA.

Bibliography

Harvard Business Review 2010, 'Idea Watch: Cloud Computing', *Harvard Business Review*, June 2010, pp. 24–30.

IDG Connect 2012, *The Global Shift to Android: Businesses & IT Professionals*, IDG Connect, June 2012, Online Available at:

Intel Corporation 2011, The New CIO Agenda: Inter Cloud Computing Insights 2011, Intel Corporation USA, pp. 1–14.

Laudon, K.C. & Laudon, J.P. 2005, *Essentials of Management Information Systems: Managing the Digital Firm*, 6th edn, Prentice Hall.

Laudon, K.C. & Laudon, J.P. 2012, *Essentials of Management Information Systems: Managing the Digital Firm*, 12th edn, Prentice Hall.

Kaplan, J. M. 2011, 'Nine questions technology leaders should be asking themselves about infrastructure', *McKinsey on Business Technology*, Number 22, Spring 2011, pp. 2–5.

Kleiner, A. 2012, 'The thought leader interview: Bob Carrigan(CEO IDG Communications)', *Strategy + Business*, Issue 66, Spring 2012, pp. 1–8.

Korkmaz, B., Lee, R. & Park, L. 2011, 'How new Internet standards will finally deliver a mobile revolution', *McKinsey Quarterly*, April 2011, pp. 1–9.

Manyika, J. 2008, 'Google's views on the future of business: An Interview with CEO Eric Schmidt', *McKinsey Quarterly*, September 2008, Online available at:
https://www.mckinseyquarterly.com/Googles_view_on_the_future_of_business_An_interview_with_CEO_Eric_Schmidt_2229

Markus, D. 2012, 'IT systems: Right size or wrong size, elastic or fixed cost: what does this all mean for IT and productivity'', *Smart Company*, July 12, 2012, Online Available at:
http://www.smartcompany.com.au/tech-strategy/right-size-or-wrong-size-elastic-or-fixed-cost-what-does-this-all-mean-for-it-and-productivity.html
(accessed Aug 20, 2012).

O'Brien, J.A. & Marakas, G.M. 2006, *Management Information Systems*, 7th edn, Irwin/McGraw-Hill, Boston.

O'Brien, J. A. & Marakas , G. M. 2011, *Management Information Systems*, 10th Edition, McGraw-Hill, New York, USA.

Pearlson, K.E. & Saunders, C.S. 2004, *Managing and Using Information Systems: A Strategic Approach*, 2nd edn, Wiley, Danvers.

Pearlson, K. E. & Saunders, C. S. 2010, *Managing and Using Information Systems: A Strategic Approach*, Fourth Edition, John Wiley & Sons, USA.

Roberts, R. & Sikes, J. 2011, 'How IT is managing new demands: McKinsey Global Survey results', *McKinsey on Business Technology*, Number 22, Spring 2011, pp. 24–33.

Roberts, R. Sarrazin, H. & Sikes, J. 2010, 'Reshaping IT management for turbulent times', *McKinsey on Business Technology*, Number 21, pp. 2–9.

Trend Micro 2010, 'The Need for cloud computing security', *Trend Micro White Paper July 2010*, Trend Micro Inc. USA, pp. 1–7.

Wang, K. W. 2010, 'Creating Competitive Advantage with IT Architecture', *McKinsey on Business Technology*, Number 18, Winter 2010, pp. 18–21.

Chapter 7

Using Information Systems for Enhancing Internal Operation: Enterprise Resource Planning Systems

In this chapter, we will review functional information systems, explain why there is a trend towards cross-functional information systems, identify the major cross-functional information systems in business and their main roles, explain the need for enterprise resource planning (ERP) systems in business, discuss implementation issues of ERP systems, and describe emerging trends of ERP systems.

7.1 Functional and Cross-functional Information Systems

Traditionally businesses are operated by dividing the organisation into various functions in a silo structure with each having its own information system and tending to work in isolation. Functional information systems consist of a variety of types of information systems (transaction processing, management information, decision support, etc.) that support the business functions of: Accounting; Finance; Marketing; Productions/operations management; Human resource management. In the real world information systems are typically integrated combinations of functional information systems (O'Brien & Marakas 2011, p. 287).

The functional (silo) approach to information systems allows organisations to optimise expertise and avoid redundancy in expertise. It also makes it easier to benchmark with other organisations, develops core competencies, and provides functional efficiency (Pearlson & Saunders 2004, p. 106; Pearlson & Saunders 2010, p. 140). However there are some problems with this approach. In order to deal with these problems of silo approach (i.e., information recreation, information errors, communication gaps among departments, loss of information arising from inaccurate information and not-timely shared information, and lack of consistent services to customers), managers need to think beyond the walls of the organisation. Thus there is a need for a cross-functional approach, which focuses on business process and customer services and is supported by cross-functional information systems that cross the boundaries of several business functions (O'Brien & Marakas 2011, p. 275). It is noted that even though we use the term of cross-functional approach, it also includes cross-channel integration (i.e., integrating online shops, physical stores, call centers and other channels to have unified and timely (or real time) shared information about the customer).

Cross-functional information systems are a strategic way to use information systems to share information resources and focus on accomplishing fundamental business processes in concert with the company's customer, supplier, partner, and employee stakeholders. Some typical examples of cross-functional information systems include: enterprise resource planning systems, customer relationship management systems, supply chain management systems, and knowledge management systems. These four systems have different focuses: enterprise resource planning systems emphasize on internal efficiency; customer relationship management systems concentrate on customer relations; supply chain management systems focus on managing relations with suppliers and business partners; and knowledge management systems facilitate managing tacit and explicit knowledge of the organization. Meanwhile these four systems are inter-related (i.e., accurate information is critical to the success of supply chain management systems and enterprise planning systems; knowledge sharing facilitated by knowledge management systems is important to all the aspect of business including the success of supply chain management systems, enterprise planning systems, customer relationship management systems).

Another two commonly used cross-functional information systems are transaction processing systems and enterprise collaboration systems. Transactions are events such as sales, purchases, deposits, withdrawals, refunds, and payments. Transaction processing systems are cross-functional information systems that capture and process data describing business transactions (O'Brien & Marakas 2011, p. 278). Enterprise collaboration systems are information systems that use a variety of information technologies to help people work together, including electronic communications tools (i.e., e-Mail, instant messaging, voice mail, faxing, web publishing, paging), electronic conferencing tools (i.e., data conferencing, voice conferencing, video conferencing, discussion forums, chat systems, electronic meeting systems), and collaborative work management tools (i.e., calendaring & scheduling, task & project management, workflow systems, document sharing, and knowledge management) (O'Brien & Marakas 2011, p. 281). Enterprise collaboration systems enhance communication (i.e. sharing information with each other), coordination (i.e. coordinating individual work efforts and use of resources with each other), and collaboration (i.e. working together cooperatively on joint projects and assignments) across the organisation (O'Brien & Marakas 2011, p. 280).

7.2 Enterprise Resource Planning Systems

7.2.1 *Evolution of enterprise resource planning systems*

Enterprise resource planning (ERP) has its origin in the material requirements planning (MRP) (to manage inventory in production) then MRPII, which are mainly for manufactures to plan all the resources for its production. Enterprise resource planning systems can be seen as an extension of MRPII systems with integrated functions/modules such as accounting and finance, human resource management, manufacturing, logistics, and distribution although nowadays ERP systems can be found in all kinds of organisations (i.e., universities, governments, service providers) including those that are not primarily involved in manufacturing. The latest version of ERP systems has included web-based ERP applications and integrated other applications/components/modules, such as supply chain management, customer relationship management, and business intelligence. Major ERP software vendors are SAP, PeopleSoft, Oracle, JD Edwards, Infor, and Microsoft.

ERP systems have been implemented in many large corporations, and more and more SMEs are embarking on ERP systems. The EPR market is large and significant, for example in 2011, the ERP systems market was worth more than US$ 36 billion (Krigsman *et al.* 2010). Haag, Baltzan and Phillips (2008, p. 136) suggest the three primary forces driving the explosive growth of enterprise resource planning systems are:

- ERP system is a logical solution to the mess of incompatible applications that had sprung up in most businesses
- ERP system addresses the need for global information sharing and reporting
- ERP system is used to avoid the pain and expense of fixing legacy systems.

7.2.2 *Business values of ERP system*

Enterprise resource planning (ERP) system is a cross-functional enterprise system that integrates and automates many of the internal business processes of a company, particularly those within the manufacturing, logistics, distribution, accounting, finance, and human resource functions of the business (O'Brien & Marakas 2011, p. 320). ERP systems track business resources and the status of commitments made by the business and give a company a real-time cross-functional view of its core business processes, such as production, order processing, and sales, and its resources, such as cash, raw materials, production capacity, and people (O'Brien & Marakas 2011, p. 333). It features a set of integrated software modules and normally a central database that allow data to be shared by many different business processes and functional areas throughout the enterprise (Laudon & Laudon 2005, p. 333). The primary purpose of an ERP system is to collect, update, and maintain enterprise-wide information, so the same information can be shared across different departments and functions of the organization. And the shared information enable different departments and function work together (so they don't work in silos).

Successful implementation of ERP systems can provide organisations with many benefits. Examples include:(O'Brien and Marakas 2011, p. 324; Haag, Baltzan & Phillips 2008, p. 398):

- Quality and efficiency enhancement by helping improve the quality and efficiency of customer service, production, and distribution by creating a framework for integrating and improving internal business processes
- Decreased costs by replacing old legacy systems, reductions in transaction processing costs and hardware, software, and information systems support staff, and reduction in inventory
- Decision support assistance through providing cross-functional information on business performance to assist managers in making better decisions
- Enhanced enterprise agility through breaking down many walls and creating a more flexible organisational structure, managerial responsibilities, work roles and integrated financial information.

7.2.3 *The costs of ERP system implementation*

Costs involved in implementing ERP systems are considerable. Hardware and software costs are a small part of the total costs. O'Brien and Marakas (2011, p. 325) point out the costs of developing new business processes (reengineering) and preparing employees for the new ERP system (training and change management) could be very high (more than 50% of the total implementation costs). Data conversion (i.e. converting from previous legacy systems to the new cross-functional ERP system) could also be very expensive. Consulting fees, process reworking, customisation, testing, and integration could also be costly. The breakdown (in percentage) of typical costs of implementing a new ERP system includes: engineering (43%), software (15%), data conversion (15%), training and change management (15%), and hardware (12%) (O'Brien & Marakas 2011, p.325). ERP system implementation costs also could be viewed from another perspective and includes up-front costs (i.e., hardware, software, consulting fees), recurring annual costs (i.e., for license and support), upgrade costs (i.e., for newer version and added functionalities), implicit costs (i.e., internal information systems resources costs), and additional costs (i.e., cloud applications, increasing security expenditure, additional support) (Krigsman *et al.* 2010). A recent survey of 63 SMEs and large firms indicates that the average total cost of ownership of an ERP system is $15 million. Total cost of ownership ranges from 400,000 to 30 million (Pearlson & Saunders 2004, p. 118; Haag, Baltzan & Phillips 2006, p. 282). Another recent study by Aberdeen group, which surveyed 1,680 manufacturing companies of all sizes, cited in Koch and Wailgum (2008), found that companies with less than US$ 50 million in revenue should expect to an average of US$ 384, 295 in total ERP system costs, just over US$ 1 million for companies with US$ 50 million to 100 million in revenue, just over US$ 3 million for companies with US$ 500 million to 1 billion in revenue, and nearly US$ 6 million for companies with more than US$ 1 billion in revenue. On a related note, on average it will take one to three years to have real transformation resulting from ERP system implementation (but the emphasis is not focusing on how long it will take but on understanding why you need it and how you will use to improve the business of the organization) (Koch & Wailgum 2008). In additional according to a 2011 ERP report produced by Panorama Consulting Solutions cited in Kimberling (2011) the average ERP system implementation time reduced to 14 months in 2010 (from 18 months in 2009) and the average total costs of ERP system implementation fell to 4.1% of implementing firms' annual revenue (from 6.1% in 2009).

7.2.4 *Challenges and issues of ERP system implementation*

ERP systems affect an entire organisation simultaneously rather than a single department as is the case with functional information systems, which are only limited to departmental boundaries (Reimers 2003). However, developing and implementing a new ERP system is definitely not as simple as installing the software package and required hardware. Properly implementing ERP systems is a difficult and costly process that has caused serious business losses for some companies, who typically underestimated the importance of planning, development, training, and required organizational adjustments. Some reported causes of ERP system implementation failures are (O'Brien & Marakas 2011, pp. 326-327; Krigsman 2010; The Authors' Own Knowledge):

- Unrealistic implementation expectations and underestimating the complexity of planning, development, training, and required organizational adjustments. failure to involve affected employees from the beginning of the implementation process.
- Trying to do too much, too fast in the conversion phase.
- Insufficient training for the new work tasks required by the ERP system.
- Failure to do enough data conversion and testing.
- Lack of ERP system implementation expertise OR over-reliance on external expertise (i.e., consultants, vendors).
- Lack of fit between ERP system and business needs: too many ERP implementation failures resulting from failed in fulfilling the real needs of the organization.
- Lack of business leaders' buy-in and support
- Have the tendency to over-customization, which either costs you very much or indicates you have chosen the wrong software. A rule of thumb for customization is less than 30% (ideally 20%).

While ERP system implementation failures could have been due to technical issues, most of the time they are due to change management and business process implementation issues (Turner 2004). ERP systems require a fundamental transformation of a company's business processes. People, processes, policies, and the company's culture are all factors that should be taken into consideration when implementing a major enterprise system (such as EPR systems). ERP systems often changes the way an organisation operates because ERP developers typically include industry best practices in the system and create the system without knowing the exact requirements of their future customers (Reimers 2003). Davenport (1998, p. 123) expresses the view that "Enterprise systems are basically generic solutions even though they integrate industry best practices in many cases. Of course some degree of customisation is possible, but major modifications are very expensive and impractical. As a result, most companies installing enterprise systems will have to adapt or rework their processes to reach a fit with the system". On the other hand, inflexibility of ERP packages may sometime lock companies into rigid processes which make it hard, if not impossible, to adapt quickly to changes in the marketplace or in the structure of the organisation. The embedded best practices in ERP packages may also not be able to apply to all businesses (Pearlson & Saunders 2004, p. 118). Many companies are still adjusting themselves to the concept of 'cross-functional integration', using a centralised database. Furthermore, while the costs and risks of failure in implementing a new ERP system could be substantial, it also takes time to realise benefits (Haag, Baltzan & Phillips 2008, p. 398).

In order to avoid ERP system implementation failures, organisations should (Turner 2004; Pearlson & Saunders 2004, p. 121; O'Brien & Marakas 2011, pp. 326-327; Blick & Quaddus 2003; Tippit 2008; Krigsman 2010; The Authors' Own Knowledge):

- Know what they want the ERP system to do and understand specific business problems the organization needs to solve with ERP implementation.
- Involve staff in the ERP project from the beginning.
- Understand change management.
- Have a balanced project management team with an unswerving project champion and develop an effective project plan to look after scope, timeframe and resources aspects of the ERP system implementation.
- Hire consultants with proven track records.
- Conduct extensive data conversion and data testing.
- Understand the very complex nature of the enterprise resource planning system implementation.
- Define realistic scope and goals.
- Gain support from top management
- Provide people with sufficient training and allocate sufficient resources
- Put in place effective ERP system performance measurement metrics and benefits realization strategy, and have designated people responsible for them.

Pearlson and Saunders (2004, pp. 119–120) point out that sometimes organisations have to make a decision between (1) letting the ERP system drive business process redesign or (2) re-designing the business process first then implementing ERP system. The former approach is suitable for new businesses, or for businesses whose processes are not sources of competitive advantage, or for businesses whose current systems are in crisis and there is not enough time, resources or knowledge within the firms to fix them. The latter approach can be applied when business processes, which have to be designed in-house not from the package, give a firm competitive advantage, or when features of available packages and the needs of businesses do not fit. On a related note, organisations also can use data warehouses (poor man's ERP) if they don't want to pay for the costs and risks involved in the ERP system implementation (Pearlson & Saunders 2004, p. 120).

Meanwhile for organizations of different sizes the emphasis of the ERP implementation could be varied, such as on-going operational support for small firms, selecting right software for mid-size firms, and integration & implementation for large firms (Krigsman et al. 2010). Furthermore as mentioned earlier, selecting a right vendor is critical to the success of ERP implementation. We look for candidates of potential ERP system suppliers, organizations could look at the following perspectives (Krigsman et al. 2010):

- Kinds of customers they typically serve: small or large?, industry?, and region?
- Appropriate references from various reliable sources.
- Process and methodology for implementation.
- Facilitating process for improvement or reengineering during the implementation.
- Approach and expertise in handling change management.
- Process for controlling project scope and budget.
- Ways of responding to identified mismatch between business requirements and software package's functionalities.
- Definition and measures of the success of implementation.
- Benefit realization strategy and execution.
- Experience and background of the proposed team members for the ERP system implementation project.

7.2.5 Integration issues

Most organisations have various systems and applications from multiple vendors. Often organisations take the approach of best-of-breed for the reason that no one vendor can respond to all an organisation's needs (Haag, Baltzan & Phillips 2008, p. 138). Organisations, which are looking for optimal solutions for individual areas, are more likely to go for the best-of-breed approach for richer functionalities.

One of the most popular integration tools is enterprise application integration (EAI) (Haag, Baltzan & Phillips 2008, p. 138). EAI is a software (a kind of middleware), which enables two business applications to communicate and to exchange data (Laudon & Laudon 2005, p. 217; O'Brien & Marakas 2011, p. 277). EAI can integrate front-office and back-office applications to allow for quicker, more effective responses to business events and customer demands, thereby improving customer and supper experience with the business. (O'Brien & Marakas 2011, p. 277). Laudon & Laudon (2005, p. 217) point out that, compared to the traditional approach of integrating where you need to have different and customised software to connect one application to another, EAI connects disparate applications and multiple systems through a single software hub using a special middleware.

7.2.6 Emerging trends of ERP Systems

In the future we will see more open and flexible software packages, such as more customisable interfaces to suit individual needs (Haag, Baltzan & Phillips 2008, p. 401). In line with the wide accessibility of the Internet and rapid development of networks and Internet technologies, more and more organizations will be looked at web-based (cloud) ERP systems (Haag, Baltzan & Phillips 2008, p. 401; O'Brien & Marakas 2011, p. 327; Krigsman et al. 2010). A mixed or hybrid model, which combines in-house deployment of ERP system components and web-based (cloud) ERP system modules, will be adopted by more and more organizations. Another future trend for ERP systems is the development of inter-enterprise ERP systems that provide web-enabled links between key business systems of a company and its customers, suppliers, distributors, and others (O'Brien & Marakas 2011, p. 327). Meanwhile, allowing users to access an organization's ERP system via mobile devices (also called enterprise mobility) will be another emerging trend (Haag, Baltzan & Phillips 2008; Krisgman et al. 2010). Social web computing capabilities to meet with the demand of exponentially growing social networks is another area organizations' ERP systems should cover. Haag, Baltzan and Phillips (2008) suggest that in the future lines between SCM, CRM, and ERP systems will continue to blur, and their view is supported by the fact that ERP vendors are adding more and more modules/components into their ERP packages(one recent emphasis is Business Intelligence as a result of the increasing importance of better understanding customers and the availability of Big Data). ERP software companies have developed modular, web-enabled software suites (e.g. oracle's E-business suite) that integrate ERP, CRM, SCM, procurement, decision support, enterprise portals, and other business applications and functions.

Although our discussion has predominantly concentrated on manufacturing businesses, ERP systems have been widely adopted in the service industry and other industries (including public sector).

Another emerging/future trend is the web-based On Demand ERP Services (i.e. renting the required ERP services rather than owning and maintaining in house). An example of On Demand ERP Services is SAP Business ByDesign, which charges fees according to usage of per user, per month for the software, infrastructure, services and support (i.e., US$149 per user per month for minimum 10 users for standard enterprise user-see more information on SAP Business (http://www.sap.com/solutions/technology/cloud/business-by-design/pricing/users.epx).

7.2.7 Second wave of ERP systems

Graham Shanks of University of Melbourne, Australia believes that the first wave of ERP was a more IS/IT view of projects: let's get the software in and working; second wave implementation will see the process more as a business project where you have the opportunity to realign your business processes, change the way you do things with IS/IT as an enabler (Turner 2004, p. 5).

While it is true that most of the Fortune 500 companies have already adopted ERP systems, the next target for growth are the small and medium enterprises (SMEs) and industry-specific solution markets. EPR software vendors have been working hard to target SMEs to install ERP systems and have released less-expensive, modular and hosted versions of their software. Vendors' strategy is to make the systems more user-friendly to SMEs so that they can avoid customisation, which can really drive up costs. SAP Business One is an example of ERP Solutions for Small and Midsize Enterprises (http://www.sap.com/solutions/sme/business-one/small-business-management-software.epx). Another cut-down version for small business is Open ERP (open source ERP system) (http://www.openerp.com).

7.3 Summary

In this chapter, we reviewed functional information systems and explained the need for cross-functional information systems, which have become very important to modern businesses. We introduced enterprise resource planning systems that are cross-functional information systems for improving internal operation, and also discussed different perspectives of ERP systems, including benefits, costs, features, implementation, trends and future directions. In the next chapter, we will have a close look at two popular cross-functional information systems for improving external relations: customer relationship management (CRM) systems and supply chain management (SCM) systems.

Bibliography

Blick, G. & Quaddus, M. 2003, *Benefit Realization with SAP: A Case Study*, Graduate School of Business, Curtin University of Technology, Australia, pp. 1–16.

Davenport, T. 1998, 'Putting the enterprise into the enterprise system', *Harvard Business Review*, July/August 1998, pp. 121–131.

Bibliography

Haag, S., Baltzan, p. & Phillips, A. 2006, *Business Driven Technology*, 1st edition, McGraw-Hill Irwin, Boston, USA.

Haag, S., Baltzan, p. & Phillips, A. 2008, *Business Driven Technology*, 2nd edn, McGraw-Hill Irwin, Boston, USA.

Kimberling, E. 2011, 'Who are top ERP vendors in 2011', *Panorama Consulting*, Online Available at: http://panorama-consulting.com/who-are-the-top-erp-vendors-in-2011/ (accessed August 20, 2012).

Koch, C. & Wailgum, T. 2008, 'ERP definition and Solutions', *CIO*, Online Available at: http://www.cio.com/article/print/40323 (accessed August 20, 2012).

Krigsman, M. 2010, 'Lessons from ERP Implementation Failures', *Focus Research*, Online Available at: http://www.ithound.com/abstract/lessons-erp-implementation-failures-6935 (accessed July 15, 2012).

Krigsman, M., Fauscette, M., Kimberling, E., Simon, p. & Sommer, B. 2010, 'The 2011 Focus Experts' Guide to Enterprise Resource Planning', *Focus Research*, Online Available at: http://www.sbaconsulting.com/research/ERP-Expert-Guide-final-4.pdf (accessed July 15, 2012).

Laudon, K.C. & Laudon, J.P. 2005, *Essentials of Management Information Systems: Managing the Digital Firm*, 6th edn, Prentice Hall.

O'Brien, J. A. & Marakas, G. M. 2011, *Management Information Systems*, 10th Edition, McGraw-Hill, New York, USA.

Pearlson, K.E. & Saunders, C.S. 2004, *Managing and Using Information Systems: A Strategic Approach*, 2nd edn, Wiley, Danvers.

Pearlson, K. E. & Saunders, C. S. 2010, *Managing and Using Information Systems: A Strategic Approach*, Fourth Edition, John Wiley & Sons, USA.

Reimers, K. 2003, 'Implementing ERP Systems in China', *Communications of the Association for Information Systems*, Vol. 11, pp. 335–356.

Tippit Inc. (2008) *Inside ERP: Midmarket ERP Solutions Buyer's Guide*, Online Available at: http://www.inside-erp.com/ (accessed July 15, 2012).

Turner, A. (2004). 'ERP Rides the Second Wave', *The Sydney Morning Herald*, 10 February, Online Available: http://www.smh.com.au/articles/2004/02/09/1076175092011.html (accessed 20 March 2006).

Chapter 8

Using Information Systems for Improving External Relations: Customer Relationship Management Systems and Supply Chain Management Systems

In this chapter, we will explain benefits from effective customer relationship management (CRM) and CRM systems, review different types of CRM applications/systems, discuss challenges & issues involved in implementing CRM systems as well as the future trends in the development of CRM systems, explain benefits from effective supply chain management (SCM) and SCM systems, review different types of SCM applications/systems, and discuss challenges & issues involved in implementing SCM systems as well as the future trends in the development of SCM systems.

8.1 Customer Relationship Management Systems

8.1.1 *The customer-focused business strategy*

A customer-focused business strategy is not a matter of choice – rather it is a matter of necessity, and technology makes this possible. Technologies, especially Internet technologies, have been increasingly used in the marketplace (market space) to reach consumers. Two great examples of winning the competition by applying customer–focused strategy are Apple and Google, both of them are focusing on user experience even though the former is more building on Steve Job's intuiting the experience of customers by putting himself into their shoes while the latter is more using data-driven and iterative approach by having and testing a lot of data to provide better products and services customers want and like (Shapiro 2012). Today's customers can quickly change from one company's product offering to that of other companies with a click of a mouse. Businesses have come to realise that the relationships that they build with cutomers are their most valuable assets (O'Brien & Marakas 2011, p. 309). The focus of competition has shifted from who sells the most products and services to who owns the customers.

8.1.1.1 *Good understanding of customers*

A critical aspect of successfully implementing customer-focused strategy is to have good understanding of customers. Organizations could develop good understanding of customers' needs via applying good research (via both qualitative and quantitative methods) on customers, gaining market insights, and using intuition based on experiences (Edelman 2010b; Shaprio 2012).

In addition, a good understanding of the customer/consumer decision journey/process and how technologies can assist in different parts/stages of the journey/process is essential as well. The customer decision journey can be grouped into three categories (Laudon & Traver 2012, pp. 397-398; Edelman 2010a, 2010b; Divol, Edelman & Sarrazin 2012; Turban *et al.* 2012, p. 433; The Authors' Own Knowledge):

- Pre-purchase activities: including awareness/need recognition (i.e., considering something because of external influences (such as advertisements, peer-influence, word of mouth) or/and actual needs), and searching for suitable products & services, and evaluation of alternative options. On top of the traditional media of TV, radio, print media, print advertisements, catalogues mass media, networks and other things (such as store visits and sales people's push), technologies/applications (especially Internet based) such as banners advertisements, interstitials, video ads, permission emails, e-newsletters, social networks, search engines, blogs & micro-blogs, online forums, online chatting, online communities, virtual/online catalogues, information intermediaries and site visits, could provide assistance in this stage.

- Purchase/Buy activities: including buying online (via firms' own sites or third-party platforms), buying in the store, paying online, and picking-up in the store, buying online via kiosks or other computing devices in the store, online payment systems, and online delivery (arrangements). Technologies/applications such as e-payment systems, e-commerce shopping sites/e-commerce systems for taking and processing online orders and online payments, e-commerce third-party trading platforms, online logistic management systems, content management systems, and online coupon and discount systems, could assist in this stage.

- Post-purchase activities: including enjoying/experiencing the product/service, advocating the product/service, having the bond with the product/service, and repurchasing the product/service. On top of traditional measures of warranties, service calls, repairs, returns, refunds, and customer groups & networks, technologies/applications such as social networks, blogs & micro-blogs, online forums, online user groups, online chatting, online communities, e-mails, newsletters, follow-ups & updates, radio frequency identification tags, online behaviour tracking and monitoring systems, business intelligence/business analytics, could be useful in this stage.

It could be argued that the Internet has been particularly useful to customers in the areas of (pre-purchase) search & evaluation and (post-purchase) reviews & advocacy. It also could be said search engines (especially Google) have been effective in helping us find information even though the results are not perfect-most of the search results (normally after first page) don't really match with what we are looking for. There is just too much information there on the web, and our (eyeball) attention is limited. Businesses that can effectively grasp our attention for information and advertisements at the right time at the right place will be doing fine. In fact, according to Hal Varian, Google's Chief Economist (reported in Manyika 2009), Google has developed its entire business model around the notion.

In addition, for the majority of businesses (at least now and in the near future) applying a mix of online and offline communications is the most effective way, and the combination of digital and non-digital channels is still the way to go (and it will be true for many years to come) since the technology is not their core business and is only used for supporting their business processes and operations. Organizations need to adopt a "omni-channel" approach (Rigby 2011), which takes advantages of both digital and non-digital channels (i.e., 24/7 availability, convenience, wider selection, easy comparison, customer reviews, social engagement for digital channel; and shopping experience, tangible feeling, personal human help, convenient return, instant access to products/services for non-digital(traditional) channel).

8.1.1.2 *Using social technologies*

Social technologies (including social networking sites, video sharing, photo-sharing, blogs & microblogs, forums, social gaming, social commerce, ratings and reviews, crowdsourcing, shared work spaces, RSS, Podcasts, and wiki applications) have been becoming popular in recent years (for example it is reported in Chui *et al.* (2012, pp. 1-2) there are more than 1.5 billion members globally for social networks (IT enabled communities), 80% of worldwide Internet users interact with social networks regularly). Meanwhile the results of a recent McKinsey survey of 4,200 executives around the world indicates (reported in Chui *et al.* 2012, pp. 1-2) 70% of participating businesses of the survey using some forms of social technologies and 90% of these firms adopting social technologies report business benefits from using them, but such results have to be interpreted with caution since such figures may not truly reflect the realities in different sectors and countries/regions, for example in the same report it is also indicated that only 31% of American SMEs used social media in 2011.

In addition, according to McKinsey Global Institute's recent surveys (reported in Bughin, Hung Bayers & Chui 2011; Chui *et al.* 2012, pp. 1-2), organizations are using social technologies for such purposes as: scanning external environment, finding new ideas, managing projects, developing strategic plan, allocating resources, matching employees to tasks, assessing employee performance, improving intra-inter-organizational collaboration and communication, providing services to customers, gathering customer insight, supporting marketing and sales activities, conducting social commerce, and determining compensation. In another McKinsey Global Institute's study (reported in Chui *et al.* 2012), it is found annual value in four sectors studied (including Financial services, Consumer package goods, Professional services, and Advanced manufacturing) could be unlocked by social technologies is between US$ 900 billion to 1.3 trillion, and furthermore social technologies have the potential to raise the productivity of knowledge workers by 20-25%.

Businesses therefore need to allocate more technology resources in these areas to attract and retain customers. Businesses have started increasingly using social networks for commercial purposes (i.e., marketing and advertising), and they believe the notion when a customer "likes" (i.e., Like function in Facebook) a company or interacts with it he/she is more likely to buy its products and services (Kleiner 2012). One related note, recently in Australia (August 2012), ACCC (Australia Consumer & Competition Commission) requested businesses in Australia to be responsible for their Facebook and Twitter pages and information (including comments) on the pages-they need to act on the misleading information and inappropriate comments on Facebook and Twitter.

8.1.1.3 *Excellent customer service*

One good example of excellent customer service is Zappo.com, which has seven practices of exceptional customer services (Hsieh 2010):

- Organizations should make customer service a priority of the whole firm.
- Organizations should empower customer service representatives/people
- Organizations should fire bad customers who are abusive and unreasonable.
- Organizations t should not measure call time, should not upsell, and should not use scripts for phone conversations with customers.

- Organizations should be keen in talking to customers: provide phone number and make it visible to customers.
- Organizations should treat cost of serving customers via phone/call centers as an investment but not an expense.
- Organizations should celebrate and share stories of exceptional customer service across the organization.

Another important dimension of customer service in today's environeent is timely and effectively addressing customers' complains and problems/service mishaps, especially on-line complains (Tripp & Gregoire 2011; Collier & Beinstock 2006). One latest example is the video clip posted on Youtube titled "United Break Guitars", which has been viewed more than 10 million times. Organizations need to quickly identify the issues and take appropriate actions (normally with quite short timeframe). They need to provide complaining customers with the opportunity to talk to a person, fair & transparent processes, policies and procedures of dealing with complains, and compensations & apologies.

According to one recent global survey of 1,469 senior executives of different sizes and from different sectors and regions (reported in Brown & Sikes 2012), some digital marketing practices adopted by firms (in the order) include:

- Positioning and branding consistently across multiple channels.
- Engaging customers socially (via social media).
- Offering personalized information or targeted offers through online channels.
- Advertising with advanced customer targeting.
- Running experiments via the firm's website.
- Developing capability to track customer behaviour across channels.
- Developing branded applications and games for online and mobile services.
- Using location-based services or promotions to attract customers to the store.

Kleiner (2012) argues since there is overload of information everywhere, and users tend to rely on trusted sources of knowledge for information, such as Wikipedia for general and subject knowledge, eBay for used items, Amazon for books, electronics and e-commerce, Google map for driving routes, and Linkedin for professional background of interested people.

According to ZenithOptimedia (cited in The Economist 2012), in 2012, Television will remain the dominant advertising medium (will account for 41% of all advertising spending and will reach US$ 200 billion in 2012) while the Internet will have the fastest growth

(15% in 2012). The advertising spending ranking of different media is TV (US$ 196 billion, 40.7%), Newspapers (91 billion, 18.9%), Internet (83 billion, 17.3%), Magazines (41 billion, 8.5%), Radio (34 billion, 7.1%), Outdoor (33 billion, 6.9%) and Cinema (3 billion, 0.6%). The 2012 growth order is Internet (15%), TV (6.1%), Outdoor (5.9%), Cinema (5.8%), Radio (3.1%), Magazines (−0.4%), and Newspapers (−1.0%).

8.1.2 Customer relationship management

Haag, Baltzan and Phillips (2008, p. 127) state that 'Customer relationship management (CRM) is a business philosophy based on the premise that those organizations that understand the needs of individual customers are best positioned to achieve sustainable competitive advantages in the future'. O'Brien and Marakas (2011, p. 309) suggest that CRM is the business focus and is an enterprise-wide effort to acquire and retain customers. It focuses on building long-term and sustainable customer relationships that add value both for the customer and the firm.

Through applying technology that collects and examines customer information from a multifaceted perspective, CRM could provide customer-facing employees with a single, complete view of every customer at every touch point and across all channels while giving the customer a single, complete view of the company (Laudon & Laudon 2005, p. 65). By applying a set of integrated applications and modules, CRM can address all aspects of the customer relationship, including customer services, sales, and marketing, provide consistent and personalised services to individual customers (mass customisation). CRM contributes to building long-term customer relations, and identifying the best and most profitable customers (Laudon & Laudon 2005, p. 65).

Laudon and Laudon (2005, p. 65) suggest that through effective customer relationship management, organisations are able to identify answers for such questions on their customers as: what is a value of a particular customer to the firm over his or her life time?, what are our most profitable customers?, who are our most profitable customers?, what do these most profitable customers want to buy?, what is the past, present and future potential of individual customers?, at what price level am I winning and losing business?, what quotes did the customer previously accept or reject?, which competitors has the customer used?, and what is the cost of shipping?. At the same time, effective customer relationship management plays an important role in business success, for example (O'Brien & Marakas 2011, p. 312):

- It costs six times more to sell to a new customer than to sell to an existing one

- A typical dissatisfied customer will tell 8 to 10 people about his/her experience
- A company can boost its profit 85% by increasing its annual customer retention by only 5%
- The odds of selling to a new customer are 15%; an old customer 50%
- 70% of complaining customers will do business with the company again if it takes care of a service mishap.

8.1.3 *Customer management relationship systems*

O'Brien and Marakas (2011, p. 309) note that customer relationship management systems are cross-functional enterprise systems that integrate and automate many of the customer serving processes in sales, marketing, and customer service. They also point out a CRM system develops an information systems framework, which integrates processes of sales, marketing, and customer service with the rest of the company's business operations, tracks all of the ways in which a company interacts with its customers, and helps analyse these interactions. CRM systems could assist in organizations' activities of acquiring new customers, enhancing relations with customers, and retaining customers (O'Brien & Marakas 2011, p. 315). Major CRM software application vendors include: Siebel, Oracle, PeopleSoft, Saleforce.com, SAP, IBM, Amdocs, and Nortel/Clarify.

Laudon and Laudon (2005, p. 406) describe a CRM system for a financial services business. The system captures customer information from all customer touch points (method of firm interaction with a customer such as telephone, email, customer service desk, conventional mail, or point-of purchase) as well as other data sources. Then it merges and aggregates the data into a single customer data repository or data warehouse where it can be used to provide better service, as well as to construct customer profiles for marketing purposes. Online analytical processing (OLAP) allows managers to dynamically analyse customer activities to identify trends or problems. Other analytical software programs (e.g. data mining) analyse aggregated customer behavior to identify profitable and unprofitable customers as well as customer activities (e.g. purchasing patterns).

CRM systems can be classified into four categories, namely operational CRM systems, analytical CRM systems, collaborative CRM systems, and port-based CRM systems (O'Brien & Marakas 2011, p. 318).

8.1.3.1 *Operational CRM applications/systems*

Operational CRM systems deal with day-to-day operations or systems that directly interact with customers (Haag, Baltzan & Phillips 2008, p. 376). Operational CRM systems can include customer-facing applications (i.e. call centres, telemarketing, telesales, tele-services, auto-responders, sales force automation) and customer-touching applications (i.e. personalised web pages, online marketing, online sales, online services, automated marketing campaigns via email, contact centre, self-tracking, self-configuration and customisation, self-information search, FAQs (Haag, Baltzan & Phillips 2008, pp. 378–384; Turban *et al.* 2006, pp. 556–561; O'Brien & Marakas 2011 p. 318).

8.1.3.2 *Analytical CRM applications/systems*

Through applying analytical marketing tools (i.e. data warehouse and data mining; OLAP) in analysing customer information and extracting vital data about customers, analytical CRM systems can assist businesses in better understanding information, better targeted marketing, and more personalised services (Haag, Baltzan & Phillips 2008, p. 384; O'Brien & Marakas 2011, p. 318; Turban *et al.* 2006, pp. 561–562). By pooling together all the data on individual customers, analytical CRM systems are able to provide a single view of each customer with information including a map of the customer's relationship with the organisation, product and usage summary, demographic and psychographic data, profitability measures, contact history summarising the customer's relationship with the business across multiple channels, marketing and sales information received by the customers (Laudon & Laudon 2005, p. 355).

Analytical CRM systems focus on such activities as (Laudon & Laudon 2005, p. 355):

(1) Developing customer segmentation strategies
(2) Developing customer profiles
(3) Analysing customer profitability
(4) Analysing product profitability
(5) Identifying cross-selling and up-selling opportunities
(6) Selecting the best marketing, service, and sales channels for each customers group
(7) Identifying trends in sales cycle length, win rate, and average deal size
(8) Analysing service solution times, service levels based on communication channel, and service activity by product line and account
(9) Analysing leads generated and conversion rates

(10) Analysing sales representatives and customer service representative productivity
(11) Identifying churn problems (i.e. measuring the number of customers who stop using or purchasing products and services from a company), among many others

8.1.3.3 Collaborative CRM applications/systems

CRM systems can be used to involve business partners, suppliers and customers in collaboratively providing better customer services, allowing greater responsiveness to customer needs, and enhancing efficiency and integration of supply chains (O'Brien & Marakas 2011, p. 318). Some examples of such systems include systems for customer self-service and feedback, and partner relationship management (PRM) systems (O'Brien & Marakas 2011, p. 318).

8.1.3.4 Portal-based CRM applications/systems

Web-based CRM portals can act as a common gateway for various levels of access to all customer information. In addition, online networking applications, such as online forums, chat rooms, usenet groups, email newsletters, and online discussion lists, can help organisations better understand and serve customers (Turban *et al.* 2006, pp. 554–555).

8.1.4 Challenges and issues of customer relationship management systems

While CRM systems can bring organisations benefits such as those stated in Haag, Baltzan and Phillips (2006, p. 114), the failure rate of CRM system implementations can be as high as 55 to 75% (Laudon & Laudon 2005, p. 357). Many companies have found CRM systems difficult to properly implement. One common and key reason for the failure of CRM systems is the lack of understanding and preparation. Some other identified reasons include (O'Brien & Marakas 2011, p. 316; Laudon & Laudon 2005, pp.357–358; Zikmund *et al.* 2003, p. 163):

- Difficulty in being able to see a 'total picture' of a customer is difficult, especially managing global customers with different languages, time zones, currencies, and regulations.
- Poor user acceptance (e.g. asking sales people to share their customer information could be hard since their income is largely based on commission. Other concerns include fears about job security and management control).
- The required shift from a product-centric view to customer centric, which could be very challenging.

- Many failures when firms try to create a cross-functional enterprise system that will integrate data from a wide array of departments into one system.
- Required changes in their culture and business processes to facilitate such cross-functional integration.
- Failures to provide proper project focus and the lack of adequate project management skills.

Failures in providing consistent services to customers from various touch points could be another reason. As per a survey conducted by Royal Bank of Canada, the largest bank in Canada, when convenience is very important to customers (i.e. convenience of online banking), what customers wanted was a bank which cares for its customers, values their businesses, and recognised them as the same individuals no matter what parts or/and which touch points of the bank they did business with (Gulati & Oldroy 2005). Organisations have to understand that CRM is more than just technology, it touches on the various aspects of the organization, and it requires enterprise-wide support. Technology itself is not able to manage customer relationships unless associated managerial and organisational issues have been properly dealt with (Laudon & Laudon 2005, p. 357).

But how to ensure a successful CRM system implementation?. Some suggestions provided by Haag, Baltzan and Phillips (2008, p. 131) include:

- Clearly communicating the CRM strategy.
- Defining information needs and flows.
- Building an integrated view of the customer.
- Implementing in iterations.
- Having scalability for organisational growth.

Gulati and Oldroy (2005), Zikmind *et al.* (2003, p. 163), and Laudon and Laudon (2005, pp. 357–358), also suggest some strategies for avoiding CRM system implementation failures. Their suggestions include:

- Conducting a survey to determine how the organisation responds to customers
- Carefully considering the components of CRM system and only choosing what you need.
- Concentrating on how CRM system can help but not too much on what it can do – place business before technology
- Deciding a strategy: refining existing processes or reengineering
- Evaluating all levels in organisations but give more attention to the front line

- Prioritising CRM system requirements classifying them into must, desired or not so important.
- Selecting appropriate CRM system from various vendors: best-of-breed approach or a single package?
- Having clear performance measures
- Adopting staged system development and phased implementation
- Gaining top management's support and commitment
- Sufficient financial commitments: total cost of ownership of the implementation can be very high.
- Making required changes in organisational culture, structure, and business processes.
- Promoting early success, carefully design the tasks involved and set up the links between units so as to minimise conflict.

8.1.5 *Future trends of customer relationship management systems*

There is no doubt that in the future CRM will continue to be a major strategic focus for companies. CRM systems no doubt will adopt new technologies such as cloud computing, mobile computing, and social computing. On-demand CRM services are emerging and are becoming more popular for benefits such as better flexibility, enhanced agility & scalability, reduced costs, and less demand for internal expertise. However data security & privacy issues will be remained as top concerns for such on-demand services provided by third parties.

8.2 Supply Chain Management Systems

8.2.1 *Supply chains*

Turban *et al.* (2006, p. 279) define supply chain as 'the flow of materials, information, money, and services from raw material suppliers through factories and warehouses to the end customers'. Supply chains have existed for thousands years. The silk road from China to other parts of the world is a good example of a very old supply chain. Laudon and Laudon (2005, p. 347) suggest that supply chains can be viewed from a push-based or pull-based perspective. The push-based model is basically the traditional build-to-stock approach while pull-based model is the strategy of build-to-order – 'make what we sell not sell what we make' (e.g. Dell computer's model).

A complete supply chain typically consists of three parts (Turban *et al.* 2006, p. 280, Haag, Baltzan & Phillips 2008, p. 118):
- Upstream supply chain: including activities of a manufacturing company with its suppliers. The major activity is procurement.
- Internal supply chain: including in-house processes for transforming the inputs from the suppliers into the outputs. Main concerns are production management, manufacturing, and inventory control.
- Downstream supply chain: including delivering the products to the final customers. And the attention is on distribution, warehousing, transportation and after-sale services.

Some typical problems along the supply chain include (Turban *et al.* 2006, p. 283):
- Slow and prone to errors because of the length of the chain involving many internal and external partners.
- Large inventories without the ability to meet demand.
- Insufficient logistics infrastructure.
- Quality problem or difficulties in controlling quality.

Lacking an effective information sharing mechanism is a major cause of failures of supply chains, and minor inaccurate information in demand could be amplified to become a much big one while it moves along the supply chain (bullwhip effect) (Laudon & Laudon 2005, p. 340).

8.2.2 *Supply chain management*

Supply chain management (SCM) is a cross-functional inter-enterprise effort that uses information systems to help support and manage the links between some of a company's key business processes and those of its suppliers, customers and business partners. Some basic elements of supply chain management include: plan, source, make, deliver, and return (Haag, Baltzan & Phillips 2008, p. 119). Through using a fast, efficient, and low cost supply chain, organisations can enhance their agility and responsiveness in meeting the demands of their customers and needs of their suppliers (O'Brien & Marakas 2011, p. 330). Some SCM benefits reported in Haag, Baltzan and Phillips (2008, p. 118) include: cost/control savings, productivity improvement, reductions in inventory levels, enhanced visibility of demand and supply, improved quality, maintaining/gaining competitive advantages. O'Brien and Marakas (2011, p. 330) and Laudon & Laudon (2005, p. 348) add some other benefits not mentioned by Haag, Batltzan and Phillips (2008), including faster, more accurate order processing, faster time to market, lower costs, and better relationships with suppliers, and better cash flow arising from supply chain efficiency.

Traditional SCM thinking involved 'I buy from my suppliers, and I sell to my customers'. Today, organisations are quickly realising the tremendous value they can gain from having visibility throughout their supply chain. Knowing immediately what is transacting at the customer end of the supply chain, instead of waiting days or weeks for this information to flow upstream, allows the organisation to react immediately (Laudon & Laudon 2005, p. 340). The role of SCM is evolving and it is not uncommon for suppliers to be involved in collaborative activities, i.e. in product development and for distributors to act as consultants in brand marketing.

8.2.3 Supply chain management systems

Supply chain management (SCM) systems, including systems for supply chain planning and systems for supply chain execution, automate the flow of information between members of a supply chain so that they can use it to make better decisions about when and how much to purchase, produce or ship (Laudon & Laudon 2005, p. 341). Supply chain planning (SCP) software can improve the flow and efficiency of the supply chain while reducing inventory by applying advanced mathematical applications. Supply chain execution (SCE) software is able to automate the different steps and stages of the supply chain (Haag, Baltzan & Phillips, p. 121).

Apart from the above mentioned supply chain planning systems and supply chain execution systems, some other technologies that can be used for managing supply chains include: extranets, intranets, corporate portals, electronic data interchange (Internet based), intra-enterprise & inter-enterprise collaboration tools, radio frequency identification tags, business to business e-business applications (i.e., buy sites, sell sites, exchanges), and many others. ,

8.2.4 Challenges and issues of supply chain management systems

Some identified challenges and issues of SCM system implementations include (Laudon & Laudon 2005, p. 349; O'Brien & Marakas 2011, p. 38; Cohen 2005):

1. Lack of proper demand planning knowledge, tools, and guidelines, which is a major source of SCM system implementation failure.

2. Inaccurate or overoptimistic demand forecasts, which will cause major production, inventory, and other business problems, no matter how efficient the rest of the supply chain management process.
3. Inaccurate production, inventory, and other business data, which is another frequent cause of SCM system implementation failures.
4. Lack of adequate collaboration among marketing, production, and inventory management departments within a company, and with suppliers, distributors, and other parties involved in the supply chain.
5. Immature SCM systems, which are hard to implement.
6. Required changes in business processes: implementation of SCM must be accompanied by improvements in the supply chain processes.
7. Firms' reluctance to share information.
8. Underestimating the amount of training: users must have in-depth knowledge of how the system works so they can properly interpret its results when they make the decisions.
9. Global supply chain issues (including geographic distances and time differences; additional costs for transportation, inventory, and local taxes; foreign government regulations; cultural differences,; varied performance standards; quality control issues; intellectual property concerns; and local talent recruitment and retention challenges).

So what are some solutions to various SCM system implementation challenges and problems? Some suggestions and industry best practices include (Haag, Baltzan & Phillips 2008 p. 123; Paulonis & Norton 2008: Cohen 2005; Lee 2004; Sheffi 2005; and Turban *et al.* 2006, pp. 284–285):

- Sharing information along the supply chain.
- Developing the trust among partners though it is not easy to achieve.
- Building relationships with your partners (especially long-term and important partners). Face-to-face communication is very important.
- Building an adaptable supply chain with the ability to spot trends and the capability to change supply chain (adaptability).
- Taking care to align the interest of all the firms in the supply chain with your own to create incentives for better performance and develop trust (alignment).
- Changing linear supply to hub structure (agility).
- Using intermediaries, who normally have access to a network of suppliers and customers, to develop new partners to complement existing ones.

- Evaluating needs of ultimate consumers not just immediate customer to avoid being a victim of the 'bullwhip effect'.
- Determining where your products stand in terms of technology cycles and product life cycles to decide approximate markets and supply chains for every product and service.
- Clearly specifying the roles, tasks, and responsibilities of all parties.
- Sharing risks, costs and rewards(i.e. compensate for the loss to retailers as a result of new product development, and buy back the excess books by publishers).
- Creating supply chains that respond to sudden and unexpected changes in markets
- Establishing supply chain collaboration: e.g. Collaborative Planning, Forecasting and Replenishment (CPFR) program; integrated product-development systems.
- Using inventories to solve problem: optimise and control inventories (i.e. only maintaining a stockpile of inexpensive but key components)
- Drawing up contingency plans and developing crisis management teams
- Integrating of IS/IT systems between suppliers and business partners
- Using Internet-based applications for sourcing, transportation, communications, and international finance for global SCM
- Effective management (both recruitment and retention) of local talent
- Monitoring economies all over the world to spot new supply bases and markets.

Laudon and Laudon (2005, p. 343) and Haag, Baltzan and Phillips (2008, p. 123) also stress the importance of the need to measure the performance of the supply chain. The measurement can be done by examining factors of fill rate (ability to fill the orders by due day), on-time deliveries, average time from order to delivery, total supply chain costs, number of delays of supply in inventory, supply chain response time, forecast accuracy and source/make cycle time, cash-to-cycle time, among many others (Laudon & Laudon 2005, p. 343).

Furthermore, Chopra and Meindi (2004, pp. 524–525) point out when organisations are making decisions on SCM systems, they should only select information systems that address a firm's key success factors (i.e. inventory in PC business (demand is unstable and short product life cycle)) versus inventory in oil company (demand is fairly stable and long product life cycle)), take incremental steps (e.g. demand planning functions then supply planning applications instead of installing a complete SCM system), align the level of sophistication with the need for sophistication (trading off between ease of implementation and the system's complexity), use information systems to support decision making but not to make decisions, and have information systems for both current needs and future needs.

8.2.5 *Future trends of supply chain management systems*

Similar to previous discussion of future trends of CRM systems, new technologies such as cloud-computing, mobile computing, and social computing, will be more adopted into supply chain management systems. In addition, integration of various internal systems and external issues wold be a major focus for future supply management systems (as well as previously discussed customer relationship management systems).

O'Brien and Marakas (2011, p. 341) believe that the trends in the use of supply chain management systems today are the adoption of three possible stages in a company's implementation of SCM systems. They are:

- First stage: improving internal supply chain processes and external processes and relationships with suppliers and customers
- Second stage: working on links among suppliers, distributors, customers, and other trading partners
- Third stage: developing and implementing collaborative supply chain management applications/systems.

8.3 Summary

In this chapter, we took a closer look at two other major cross-functional information systems of CRM systems and SCM systems. We discussed their benefits, roles, challenges, and future trends. In the next chapter, we will discuss information systems for decision making.

Bibliography

Berman, S.J. & Bell, R. 2011, 'Digital Transformation: Creating New Business Models Where Digital Meets Physical', *IBM Global Business Service Executive Report*, IBM Institute for Business Value, pp. 1–17.
Brown, B. & Sikes, J. 2012, 'Minding your digital business', *McKinsey Global Survey Results*, McKinsey & Company 2012, pp. 1–9.
Bughin, J, Hung Byers, A & Chui, M 2011, 'How Social Technologies Are Extending the Organization', *McKinsey Quarterly*, November 2011, pp. 1–10.
Chopra, S. & Meindl, p. 2004, *Supply Chain Management: Strategy, Planning, and Operations*, 2nd edn, Prentice Hall, New Jersey.
Cohen. S. 2005, 'Moving to China', *Supply Chain Strategy (a news letter of Harvard Business Review)*, Vol. 1, No. 2, pp. 4–6.
Chui, M. & Fleming, T. 2011, 'Insight P & G's Digital Revolution', *McKinsey Quarterly*, November 2011, pp. 1–11.

Bibliography

Chui, M., Manyika, J., Bughin, J., Dobbs, R., Roxburgh, C., Sarrazin, H., Sands G. & Westergren, M. 2012, *The Social Economy: Unlocking Value and Pproductivity through Social Technologies*, McKinsey Global Institute, July 2012, pp. 1-170.

Collier, JE & Beinstock, CC 2006, 'How do Customers Judge Quality in an E-tailer?' *MIT Sloan Management Review*, Vol. 48, No. 1, pp. 35–40.

Divol, R., Edelman, D. & Sarrazin, H., 2012, 'Demystifying social media', *McKinsey Quarterly*, April 2012, pp. 1-11.

Edelman, DC 2010(a), 'Branding in Digital Age', *Harvard Business Review*, December 2010, pp. 62–69.

Edelman, DC 2010(b), 'Four Ways to Get More Value from Digital Marketing', *McKinsey Quarterly*, March 2010, pp. 1–8.

Gulati, R. & Oldroyd, J.B. 2005, 'The Quest for Customer Focus', *Harvard Business Review*, April 2005, pp. 92–101.

Haag, S., Baltzan, p. & Phillips, A. 2008, *Business Driven Technology*, 2nd edn, McGraw-Hill Irwin, Boston, USA.

Heish, T. 2010, 'Zappo's CEO on Going to Extremes for Customers', *Harvard Business Review*, July-August 2010, pp. 41–45.

Laudon, K.C. & Laudon, J.P. 2005, *Essentials of Management Information Systems: Managing the Digital Firm*, 6th edn, Prentice Hall.

Laudon, K.C. & Traver, C.G. 2012, *E-commerce in 2012: Business, Technology, Society*, 7th edn, Addison Wesley, Boston, USA.

Lee, H. L. 2004, 'The Triple-A Supply Chain', *Harvard Business Review*, October 2004, pp. 102–112.

Kleiner, A. 2012, 'Brand transformation on the Internet', *Strategy + Business*, June 25, 2012, Online Available at: http://www.strategy-business.com/article/00117?pg=all (accessed July 20, 2012).

Kleiner, A. 2012, 'The thought leader interview: Bob Carrigan (CEO IDG Communications)', *Strategy + Business*, Issue 66, Spring 2012, pp. 1–8.

Manyika, J. 2009, 'Hal Varian on how the Web challenges managers', *McKinsey Quarterly*, January 2009, On-line available at: https://www.mckinseyquarterly.com/Strategy/Innovation/Hal_Varian_on_how_the_Web_challenges_managers_2286 (accessed July 23, 2012).

O'Brien, J. A. & Marakas, G. M. 2011, *Management Information Systems*, 10th Edition, McGraw-Hill, New York, USA.

Paulonis, D. & Norton, S. 2008, 'McKinsey global survey results: Managing global supply chains', *McKinsey Quarterly*, July 2008, pp. 1–9.

Rigby, D. 2011, 'The Future of Shopping', *Harvard Business Review*, December 2011, pp. 65–76.

Shapiro, A. 2012, 'Are you making the most of your company's software layer', *McKinsey Quarterly*, April 2012, pp. 1–6.

Sheffi, Y. 2005, 'Creating Demand-Responsive Supply Chains', *Supply Chain Strategy (a news letter of Harvard Business Review)*, Vol. 1, No. 2, pp. 1–4.

The Economist (2012), 'The world in figures: industries', The World in 2012, *The Economist*, January 2012, pp. 117–118.

Trip, T.M. & Gregoire, Y. 2011, 'When Unhappy Customers Strike Back on the Internet', *MIT Sloan Management Review*, Vol. 52, No. 3, pp. 37–44.

Turban, E., King, D., Viehland, D. & Lee, J. 2006, *Electronic Commerce 2006: A Managerial Perspective*, International edn, Prentice Hall, Upper Saddle River, NJ.

Turban, E., King, D., Lee, J.K., , Liang, T.P. & Turban, D. 2012, *Electronic Commerce 2012: A Managerial and Social Networks Perspective*, International edn, Prentice Hall, Upper Saddle River, NJ.

Zikmund, W.G., McLeod, R. Jr. & Gilbert, F.W. 2003, *Customer Relationship Management: Integrating Marketing Strategy and Information Technology*, John Wiley, Danvers, MA.

Chapter 9

Using Information Systems for Supporting Decision Making

In this chapter, we will explain the importance of information quality for decision making, review various information systems for decision support, discuss business intelligence/business analytics, and discuss management challenges involved in developing information systems for enhancing decision making.

9.1 Enabling the Organization-Decision Making

Organisations today can no longer use a 'cook book' approach to decision making. In order to succeed in business today, companies need information systems that support the diverse information and decision-making needs of their operations. The rapid development of the Internet and other information technologies has further strengthened the role of information systems for decision-making support (Haag, Baltzan & Phillips 2008, p. 103; O'Brien & Marakas 2011, p. 390). Providing information and support for all levels of management decision making is no easy task. For example, by surveying 4,000 senior executives of across the world, the researchers from The Economist Intelligence Unit identified three most important areas information systems needs to improve upon for better management decision making (reported in The Economist Intelligence Unit 2005):(1) getting the right information at the right time; (2) ensuring access to information anywhere (and any time); and (3) sending instant alerts on things going wrong. In one recent McKinsey Global Survey of 864 executives from different industries and regions (reported in Roberts & Sikes 2011), the lack of required data is identified as the most frequently cited barrier to data-driven decision making, and other mentioned barriers include (in the order): firm's culture of prioritizing experience over data, the lack of skills in translating and synthesizing the results of data analysis for decision-making, the lack of analytical skills required to carry out analyses, litter or no interest in changing decision-making processes, and the unawareness of available data in the company. Therefore, information systems must be designed to

J. Xu and M. Quaddus, *Managing Information Systems*,
DOI: 10.2991/978-94-91216-89-3_9, © Atlantis Press 2013

produce a variety of information products to meet the changing needs of decision-makers throughout an organisation, which can be highlighted as delivering right information to right people at right time.

What is the value of information? The answer to this important question varies depending on how the information is used (Haag, Baltzan & Phillips 2008, p. 104). Two people looking at the exact same piece of information could extract completely different value from the information depending on the tools they are using to look at the information. Consider what characteristics would make information valuable and useful to you? One way to answer this question is to examine the attributes of information quality. Quality information is accurate, timely and easy to understand (O'Brien & Marakas 2011, p. 323).

Meanwhile quality information is very critical. Without quality information, making right decision is a mission impossible. Some characteristics of quality information include (Haag, Baltzan & Phillips 2008, p. 387): accuracy (determining if all values are correct), completeness (determining if any values are missing), consistency (ensuring that aggregate or summary information is in agreement with detailed information), uniqueness (ensuring that each transaction, entity, and event is represented only once in the information), and timeliness (determining if the information is current with respect to the business requirement).

Some sources of low quality information include (Mayer & Schaper 2010; Chui & Fleming 2011; Bloomberg Businessweek Research Services 2011; Milley & Wood 2010; Haag, Baltzan & Phillips 2008, p. 388; The Authors' Own Knowledge): (1) errors in collecting information (i.e., customers intentionally enter inaccurate information to protect their privacy), entering information (i.e., call centre operators enter abbreviated or erroneous information by accident or to save time), and data collection design (i.e., asking wrong questions to wrong targeted groups); (2) information from different systems with different information entry standards and formats; (3) missing information as a result of wrongly designed systems; (4) inconsistent and inaccurate information from various external and internal sources in different formats; (5) potential valuable not shared information, which is trapped in the organization silos; (6) the loss of information lost in transit from one system to another or lost in poorly integrated systems; and (7) presenting information in user unfriendly formats.

9.2 Information Systems for Decision Support

O'Brien and Marakas (2011, p. 393) suggest that the types of information required by directors, executives, managers and members of self-directed teams are different, and are directly related to the levels of management decision making involved (i.e. strategic, tactical and operational levels) and the structure of the decision situations they face (i.e. unstructured, semi-structured and structured). Laudon and Laudon (2005, p. 91) have a similar view and believe that organisations should use different kinds of information systems at the various organisational levels to support different types of decisions.

Various technologies and systems that people can use to help make decisions and solve problems are now available. In the following sections, we are going to discuss some of the systems that organisations can use for supporting decision-making. Some widely adopted decision-making information systems include management information systems, decision support systems, geographical information systems, group decision support systems, online analytical processing, executive information systems, artificial intelligence, data mining, among many others.

9.2.1 *Management information systems and decision support systems*

Management information systems were originally developed to serve middle level managers' information needs and support their decision making (Laudon & Laudon 2005, p. 47). Management information systems primarily provide information on the firm's performance to assist managers monitor and control the business operation and produce information products that support many of the day-to-day decision-making needs of managers and business professionals. They typically produce summary and exception reports based on data extracted and summarised from transaction processing systems.

O'Brien and Marakas (2011, p. 397) define decision support systems as 'computer-based information systems that provide interactive information support to managers and business professionals during the decision-making process'. Although decision support systems also serve the management level of the organisation, there are differences between these management information systems and decision support systems in four dimensions (O'Brien & Marakas 2011, p. 395):

• Decision support provided: information about the performance of the organization by management information systems versus information and decision support models (i.e.,

what-if analysis, sensitivity analysis and goal-seeking analysis) to analyse specific problems/opportunities by decision support systems.
- Information form and frequency: periodic, exception, demand and push information by management information systems versus interactive inquires and responses by decision support systems.
- Information format: pre-specified and fixed format by management information systems versus ad hoc, flexible, and adaptable format by decision support systems.
- Information processing methodology: extracting and manipulating data by management information systems versus analytical modelling by decision support systems.

9.2.2 Geographical information systems

A geographic information system is a type of decision support systems, and it applies data visualisation technology and uses geographic databases to construct and display maps and other graphic displays that support decisions affecting the geographic distribution of people and other resources (O'Brien & Marakas 2011, p. 405). Some examples are calculating emergency response times, identifying the best locations for ATM machines, finding locations for a restaurant chain, etc.

9.2.3 Online analytical processing (OLAP)

Online Analytical Processing (OLAP) applications assist managers and analysts in interactively assessing and analysing large amounts of data from multiple perspectives (O'Brien & Marakas 2011, p. 401). Sometimes this is called multidimensional data analysis, which gives an unlimited view of multiple relationships in large quantities of data. An OLAP session happens online in real time and responds to managers' queries rapidly. Online analytical processing involves several basic analytical operations including (O'Brien & Marakas 2011, pp. 406-407):
- Consolidation: Aggregation of data (sales office to region)
- Drill down: Displaying detailed data (sales by product)
- Slicing and dicing: Looking from different viewpoints to help analyse trends and patterns.

9.2.4 *Group decision support systems*

A Group Decision Support System (GDSS) is 'an interactive computer-based system to facilitate the solution of unstructured problems by a set of decision makers working together as a group' (Laudon & Laudon 2005, p. 427). The number of attendees is normally 4–5 but can increase while productivity increases. GDSS fosters a more collaborative atmosphere, increases the number of ideas generated, and can lead to more participative and democratic decision making. It employs software tools that follow structured methods for organising and evaluating ideas and preserving the results of meetings (Laudon & Laudon 2005, p. 429).

9.2.5 *Executive information systems/executive support systems*

Executive information systems /Executive support systems concentrate on meeting the strategic information needs of top management by analysing external and internal aggregate data(such as gathering competitive intelligence, monitoring corporate performance) (Laudon & Laudon 2005, p. 49). Some benefits of executive information systems (Laudon & Laudon 2005 p. 431) include:

- Flexibility in assisting decision-making: using the system as an extension of executives' own thinking process.
- The ability to analyse, compare, and highlight trends: allowing users to look at more data in less time with greater clarity.
- More easily monitoring organisational performance (i.e. via balanced score card systems) or identifying strategic problems.
- Very useful for environment scanning and providing business intelligence to help management detect strategic threats or opportunities from the environment.
- Improving management performance and extend upper management's span of control: overseeing more people with fewer resources.

Executive support systems can be configured to summarise and present key performance indicators to senior managers in the form of 'digital dashboard' or 'executive dashboard', which integrates information from multiple components and present it in a unified display (Haag, Baltzan & Phillips 2008, p. 107; Laudon & Laudon 2005, p. 432). Typically a digital dashboard will present all of the critical company information in a single screen view. The results can be displayed as graphs and charts in a web-page format, providing a page-view of all the critical information for executive decision-making (Laudon & Laudon 2005, p. 432). A picture is worth a thousand words.

Many companies now are also implementing balanced scorecard systems to support their executives to make decisions. The balanced scorecard approach supplements traditional financial measures with measures from additional perspectives, such as customers, internal business processes, learning, and growth. Executives can use balanced scorecard systems to examine how well the firm is meeting its strategic goals (Laudon & Laudon 2005, p. 433).

The key for executive information systems is to help top management easily access important internal and external information for managing an organization, and they should be able to effectively deliver varying levels of details according to the demands (i.e., navigation facilities to zoom in and zoom out the many layers of information collected by various information systems). The current offering of providing top-line view of business only by many dashboard vendors is not sufficient in this regard.

9.2.6 *Artificial intelligence technologies*

Artificial intelligence (AI) aims to develop computers that can think, reason, learn, see, hear, walk, talk, and feel (Haag, Baltzan & Phillips 2008, p. 109; O'Brien & Marakas 2011, p. 418). Although AI does not exhibit the breadth, complexity, originality, and generality of human intelligence, it plays an important role in decision making. O'Brien and Marakas (2011) suggest that artificial intelligence can be classified into three domains: cognitive science (i.e., expert systems, learning systems, fuzzy logic, genetic algorithms, neural networks, intelligent agents); robotics (visual perception, tactility, dexterity, locomotion, navigation); and natural interfaces (natural languages, speech recognition, multisensory interfaces, and virtual reality) (O'Brien & Marakas 2011, pp. 422). Three most common AI applications are expert systems (looking at imitating the reasoning process of human experts), neutral networks (modelling after human brain's mesh-like network), and intelligent agents (such as search engines).

9.2.7 *Data mining for decision support*

Data mining software analyses the vast stores of historical business data that have been prepared for analysis in corporate data warehouses, and tries to discover patterns, trends, and correlations hidden in the data that can help a company improve its business performance (Haag, Baltzan & Phillips 2008, p. 82; O'Brien & Marakas 2011, p. 410). As discussed previously data-mining often works with data warehouses. Some common types of data-mining analysis capabilities include: cluster analysis (a technique used to classify information into mutually exclusive groups), association detection (examining the degree to which variables are related and the nature and frequency of these relationships in the information), and statistical analysis (looking at functions such as information correlations, distributions, calculations, and variance analysis).

9.3 Business Intelligence/Business Analytics

Business intelligence (also called business analytics) basically refers to effectively applying data analysis for assisting business decision making. Business intelligence is not only a software solution as perceived by many business executives (Campbell, Kurtzman & Michaels 2011), it is a way of doing business in terms of intelligently utilizing information resources of the organization for improving business performance or/and creating competitive advantage. The successful implementation of business intelligence relies on broad and cross-functional support across the organization and beyond the organization (i.e., closely working with partners and strategic alliances to ensure the success of business intelligence). And comparing to other enterprise (cross-functional) information systems (such as ERP systems, CRM systems, SCM systems, KM systems), business intelligence could be more for assisting strategic level decision making even though it collects the information from various sources and requires input across the organization, and could be used more for understanding and responding to external and internal environment intelligently.

Some identified benefits of adopting business intelligence include (Milley & Wood 2010; Bloomberg Businessweek Research Services 2011):

- Obtaining key customer information (i.e., finding out most profitable customers; patterns of purchase; characteristics of segments).
- Accelerating innovation.
- Optimizing supply chains and pricing.
- Identifying the true drivers of financial performance.
- Improving the decision-making process.
- Speeding up the decision-making process.
- Better resources allocation (i.e., alignment with business strategies).
- Achieving cost efficiencies.
- Better responding to customer demands and user needs.

- Assisting in managing risks.

Some critical factors for the success of business intelligence include (Mayer & Schaper 2010; Chui & Fleming 2011; Campbell, Kurtzman & Michaels 2011; Bloomberg Businessweek Research Services 2011; The Authors' Own Knowledge):

- Managing the culture: organizations need to remove the disconnected communications between different departments as well as between business and information systems sections, encourage & then request people to use available business intelligence capabilities in their work, and establish responsibilities of ensuring the quality of information collected and processed.
- Having the support from top management: without the support from the top, fostering a pro-business intelligence culture is impossible. And senior executives need to actively use the business intelligence and have more emphasis on fact-based and data-driven decision-making.
- Having the right technology: organizations need to have the right technology for business intelligence to deal with the Big Data from various internal and external sources in different formats. Only having old technologies (such as Excel Spreadsheet) will not make them up to the challenge of Big Data. Some analytic tools they can use include: Business Reporting/KPIs/Dashboards, Forecasting, Data and Text Mining, Query and Analytics, Simulations and Scenario Development, Web Analytics, Optimization, Model Management, Interactive Data Visualization, and Social Media Analytics.
- Managing the talent: generally speaking, there is a lack of supply of the talent in business intelligence areas since it is still quite a new phenomenon. Recruiting and retaining people with business intelligence skills (i.e., actively seeking exploring right data to make discoveries) is critical, at the same time, organizations need to develop talent internally.
- Working on process: organizations need to have a transparent process for business intelligence. The expectations, investments and procedures/flows must be clearly articulated and communicated across the organization. According to Gartner Inc., an IT advisory firm, through 2012 35% of top 5,000 global companies will regularly fail to make right decision as a result of lacking the right information, processes and tools (Cited in Campbell, Kurtzman & Michaels 2011).
- Ensuring data quality (consistence and accuracy is the key) and data access for people who need

9.4 Management Challenges

Laudon and Laudon (2005, p. 414) argue that while various information systems for decision making are now available, developing information systems that can actually fulfill executive information requirements is not a simple task. The reasons are:

(1) Information systems have difficulties in supporting unstructured and fluid senior management decision-making.
(2) Senior management may not fully understand its own actual information needs (such as disagreement on critical success factors, misunderstanding strategic issues).

They suggest that there is an urgent need to create meaningful reporting and management decision-making processes for managers to access information from different systems (i.e., enterprise systems and data warehouses). And major changes in management thinking is required to maximise data advantage (i.e. asking better questions about the data, establishing better information reports and decision making processes) (Laudon & Laudon 2005, p. 414).

In addition, while managers need to effectively use information systems to work, they need to understand the danger of overreliance on electronic communication. We may have more connections via networks today, but fewer relations, less physical interactions, and insufficient "soft information" (i.e., gestures, tone of voice) (Mintzberg & Todd 2012). In addition, it should be emphasized that even though information systems could providing support to our decision, it is We-human beings- are making decision; and our intuition, experience, sense and judgment, which are essential for effective decision making, will not be placed by machines and systems.

One related note is a number of studies have indicated that the always-on and multitasking working environment, which is typical to many business executives, is so distracting and causing productivity loss (Davenport 2010). Furthermore even though organizations should pay more attention to fact-based/data driven decision-making as a result of Big Data and the available advanced analytics tools, it is argued that intuition based on working experience is still the driving factor of business decision, while the level of contribution by business intelligence could be varied as per the organizational context (i.e., from the rate of 60%/40% for traditional mix of intuition/fact-based decision making to less 60% but bigger than 50% for intuition/bigger than 40% but less than 50% for data-driven) (Bloomberg Businessweek Research Services 2011).

9.5 Summary

In this chapter, we covered a range of systems developed to assist in decision making, including management information systems, decision support systems, executive information systems, business intelligence, and other applications. Management challenges associated with developing information systems for supporting decision making are also discussed. In the next chapter, we will look at how organizations can manage their information systems operations/functions.

Bibliography

Bloomberg Businessweek Research Services 2011, *The Current State of Business Analytics: Where Do We Go from Here?*, Bloomberg 2011, pp. 1–14.

Campbell, J., Kurtzman, K. & Michael, A. 2011, 'Crafting Best-in-Class Business Intelligence', *Strategy + Business*, Issue 63, Summer 2011, pp. 1–3.

Chui, M. & Fleming, T. 2011, 'Inside P & G's digital revolution', *McKinsey Quarterly*, November 2011, pp. 1–11.

Davenport, T. H. 2010, 'Rethinking knowledge work: A strategic approach', *McKinsey on Business Technology*, Number 21, Winter 2010, pp. 26–33.

Haag, S., Baltzan, P. & Phillips, A. 2008, *Business Driven Technology*, 2nd edn, McGraw-Hill Irwin, Boston, USA.

Laudon, K.C. & Laudon, J.P. 2005, *Essentials of Management Information Systems: Managing the Digital Firm*, 6th edn, Prentice Hall.

Mayer, J. H. & Schaper, M. 2010, 'Data to dollars: Supporting top management with next-generation executive information systems', *McKinsey on Business Technology*, Number 18, Winter 2010, pp. 12–17.

Milley, A. & Wood, A. 2010, *Business Analytics Essentials*, SAS Institute Inc., pp. 1–2.

Mintzberg, H. & Todd, P. 2012, 'The Offline Executive', *Strategy+Business*, July 16, 2012, Online Available at: http://www.strategy-business.com/article/00121?pg=all&tid=27782251 (accessed July 18, 2012).

O'Brien, J. A. & Marakas, G. M. 2011, *Management Information Systems*, 10th Edition, McGraw-Hill, New York, USA.

Roberts, R. & Sikes, J. 2011, 'How IT is managing new demands: McKinsey Global Survey results', *McKinsey on Business Technology*, Number 22, Spring 2011, pp. 24–33.

The Economist Intelligence Unit 2005, *Business 2010: Embracing the Challenges of Change*, The Economist Intelligence Unit 2005, pp. 1–32.

Chapter 10
Information Systems Operation Management

In this chapter, we will discuss the importance of effectively managing enterprise IS/IT operation/function, present some popular frameworks of enterprise IS/IT operation management, discuss outsourcing options, emphasize the challenge and issues associated with outsourcing information systems, highlight the importance of effectively managing global information systems operation, and look at some popular approaches of managing global information systems operation.

10.1 Enterprise Information Systems Operation Management

Information systems are not only an essential component of business success for companies today but also a vital business resource that must be properly managed. There are many questions that require answers, such as (O'Brien & Marakas 2011, p. 595):

- How should information systems resources be managed?
- Should there be only one information systems function? Or dispersed within functional areas?
- Decentralised or centralised computer resources?
- How much should we spend on information systems?
- Which business processes should receive our information systems dollars?
- Which information systems capabilities need to be companywide?
- How good do our information systems services really need to be?
- What security and privacy risks will we accept?
- Whom do we blame if information systems fail?

These kinds of questions have to be properly addressed for the successful information systems management by the senior management.

Managing information systems is not an easy task. Many businesses have not been successful in managing their use of information systems. We have seen many information systems project failures, and information systems have not always delivered. O'Brien and Marakas (2011, p. 593) suggest the following reasons for failures of information systems:

(1) Information systems are not being used effectively (i.e. using primarily to computerise traditional business processes, rather than creating innovative business processes)
(2) Information systems are not being used efficiently (i.e. providing poor response times, frequent down times and inappropriate management of application development projects).

Some other reasons include: a lack of strategic information systems planning; a lack of top management's involvement in the planning process of information systems strategy; a lack of understanding between end users, information systems professionals, and management; the inability to manage information systems specialists, end users and projects; technology-driven business instead of business-driven technology approach, among many others. How should information systems be managed? One popular approach, proposed by O'Brien and Marakas (2011, p. 583), to managing information systems for a large organisation, includes three major elements:

1. Managing the joint development and implementation of business/information systems strategies: aligning information systems with strategic business goals

2. Managing the development and implementation of new business/information systems applications and technologies: managing the processes of information systems development and implementation, as well as exploring new opportunities arising from the development of information systems

3. Managing information systems organisation and infrastructure: managing the information systems infrastructure (including hardware, software, databases, telecommunications, networks, and other IT resources).

Keep in mind that there are no quick and easy answers for the problems in IS/IT management. However O'Brien and Marakas (2011, p. 594-595) argue that extensive and meaningful involvement by managers and end users, backed up by favourable policies and governance structures, is vital to the success and performance of information systems. With the participation of managers and end users, organisations can achieve better value of investments in information systems and enhance people's acceptance and use of information systems.

Fred and Stoddard (2004) suggest three principles of successful information systems management:
- A long term plan: need a long-term, disciplined, strategic view, and a focus on achieving the company's most fundamental goals or corporate goals. To achieve this, a good approach of information systems demand management, which has been adopted by Toyota for managing and improving its information systems function, could be very useful (reported in Cooper & Nocket 2009). This approach basically manages information systems projects as per the overall corporate needs rather than focusing on disparate needs and treating each business unit as an independent effort that creates lot of duplications and drives up unnecessary costs significantly(for example in Toyota only systems that fit with its strategic direction will be given green light).
- A unifying platform to connect and integrate various systems, applications, technologies, and data sources. Sufficient discipline and resources are needed to develop such platform.
- A high-performance information systems culture: A cohesive and pro-performance culture with clearly defined rules and sound performance management system

Roberts, Sarrazin and Sikes (2010) suggest a dual-model approach for information systems management. Their suggested model includes "Factory information systems" and "Enabling information systems' models/parts. The former emphasizes improving productivity and cost performance by utilizing lean management techniques and adopting advances & computing technology and software development (such as cloud computing and agile development), and the latter pays close attention to building organization's innovation, learning and value creation abilities by embedding flexible and focused information systems workgroups.

Lean management approach aims at creating an environment, in which initiatives such as improvements of performance and skills, waste & inefficiency reduction, and elimination efforts occur continuously. Lean management approach powers information systems management via (1) standard work practices to improve quality, consistency, and response times; (2) performance transparency for bettering measuring project progress, prioritizing tasks, and meeting targets thus developing better visibility and trust between information systems and business; (3) demand management to better utilization of resources and fewer interruptions; and (4) skills development for information systems employees and knowledge sharing among information systems employees (Bensemhoun, Chartrin & Kropf 2011). Measures such as performance management, feedback sessions, user experience surveys, formal rewards, and people development are important factors for shaping people's continuous-improvement mind-set (Chartrin 2011).

Factory information systems model is working on taking advantage of scale, standardization, and simplification of information systems in the organization to drive efficiency, operational excellence and cost savings while enabling model of information systems model is looking at making organizations more effective in responding to changes/uncertainties and developing competitive advantages through innovation and growth. The bulk of the information systems management activities should be in the aspect of Factory information systems management, and the cost savings achieved by Factory information systems model could be used to fund Enabling information systems management. The Google's rule of 80/20 (Google allows employees to spend 20% of their time in pursuing their interested projects) for time allocation could be a good starting point for the distribution of the resources for these two information systems management models (i.e., 80% resources for Factory information systems management and 20% for Enabling information systems management).

10.1.1 *Information systems governance*

Information systems governance, which is a very important concept for effective information systems management even though its importance is only recognized by many organizations in recent years, looks at such perspectives as (Weill 2004, p. 5):
- Information systems principles: high level statements about how information systems are used in the business
- Information systems architecture: an integrated set of technical choices to guide the organization in satisfying business needs. The architecture is a set of policies and rules for the use of information systems, and plots a migration path to the way business how information systems matters (such as data, technology, and applications) will be done. information systems infrastructure strategies: strategies for the base foundation of information systems (both technical and human)
- Business application needs: specifying the business needs for purchased or internally developed information systems
- Information systems investment and prioritization: decision about how much and where to invest information systems projects including project approvals and justification techniques

Meanwhile information systems decisions are made stakeholders such as (1) business monarchy including a group of, or individual, business executives (i.e., CXOs) and communities comprised of senior business executives (may include CIO but exclude information systems executives acting independently); (2) information systems monarch including individual or groups of information systems executives; (3) feudal including business unit leaders, key process owners or their delegates; (4) federal including C level executives and at least one other business group (i.e., CXO and business unit leaders)-information systems executives may be an additional participant (something like in Australia and the U.S., the federal government works with state governments to run the country); (5) information systems duopoly including information systems executives and one other group (i.e., CXO or business unit leaders), and (6) anarchy including each individual user (Weill 2004, p. 5). Meanwhile business and information systems have to be strategic partners-information systems people should be "business strategists" and "You are in this with me, Mr or Ms Business. Let us work together to manage and deliver your project" (Cooper & Nocket 2009, p. 3).

Through effective information systems governance, organizations can address problems such as: (1) disconnection between information systems strategy and business strategy; (2) information systems not meeting or supporting compliance requirements; (3) poor information systems investment management; (4) information systems service issues and operational concerns; (5) information systems staff issues (i.e., insufficient number of staff, inadequate skills); (6) outsourcing issues; (7) knowledge management challenges; (8) lack of agility/development problems; (9) insufficient disaster recovery or/and business continuity measures, and (10) security and privacy threats (Applegate, Austin & Soule 2009, p. 413).

10.1.2 *Information systems skills/talent management*

Another critical dimension of successful information systems operation management is information systems staff planning-recruiting, training and retaining good information systems staff. Agarwal et al. (2006) suggest in order to retain good information systems staff, organizations need to work on such areas as: work environment, career development, community-building initiatives, money incentives and employment incentives. One emerging trend is to hire and develop digital workforce, who have the skills to access, organize, understand, analyse, communication, and utilize the large volume of data for decision-making and for creation of new ideas (Chui & Fleming 2011; Manyika 2009).

In line with the rapid development of computing technologies, the wide penetration of the Internet, and the large scale adoption of digitization (by individuals, businesses, communities, governments), the demand for information systems skills and talent will be no doubt increasingly dramatically, and we need more information systems skills and talent. The shortage of information systems skills and talent has not been commonly recognized, which could be a major hindering factor for our future developments. The recent survey of 3,169 respondents from 105 countries by IDG Connect (2011) has highlighted this concern, and most of the participants of the survey indicated there is a lack of senior technical skills in the market. The survey also asked the respondents' opinions for information systems employment problems in their area, some reasons identified from the survey include:

- Economy uncertainty: in bad times, hiring is always slow.
- Poor training: the results of the survey indicate information systems training issue is more for of an issue for participants from developing countries in Asia, Middle East, Africa, and South America. In fact, many universities and colleges around the world that used to offer information systems training programs downsized or even closed down their information systems faculties/departments after year 2000.
- IT talent brain-drain issues: the survey results indicate it is a major issue (more than 50% participants believed) for Africans, South Americans and Asians. It has been an ongoing issue for developing countries. Their best information systems talent prefer to go overseas for better pay or/and working conditions. But in recent years, to some extent, it has changed. For example, many information systems talents in China now would stay in China as a result of rapidly rising pay and much more opportunities in China.
- The challenge of updating skills constantly as a result of a very changing information systems industry: this issue is really making people in Asia to think twice when they are planning to embark on information systems careers. In additional, the need for soft skills (i.e., interpersonal & communication, project management, language skills) was also pointed out by some respondents. It is, in fact, really true in reality. In addition, the challenge of updating skills constantly coupling with factors such as poor information systems training and information systems talent brain-drain could lead to the identified shortage of senior technical skills.
- Generation Y work ethics: the majority of respondents across all regions agree that Generation Y information systems professionals (at the entry level) have different work ethics to older generations.

Information Systems Operation Management 155

Another concern associated with information systems skills and talent management is the lack of soft skills among the information systems people who highly (if not overly) enjoy their technical skills. But information systems people don't work alone in the organization, and they are there to work with business side of the organization and are an integral part of the organization. Organizations could equip information systems people with such skills as effective working habits, better emotional intelligence and enhanced skills of persuading and influencing people to make them more communication-minded.

10.1.3 *The roles of Chief Information Officer*

Chief information officer (CIO) plays critical role in the success of IT in supporting and enabling the business. Boochever, Park and Weinberg (2002) suggest CIO should have four roles in the organization:

- A strategist who is a member of senior executive, and contributes to the development of business strategy (and associated information systems strategy), especially via leveraging on opportunities and dealing with risks associated with technologies.
- A business advisor who works closely with business unit leaders and translates information systems capabilities for business processes and operations.
- An information systems executive who is responsible for skills, training, assets, investment, performance of information systems.
- An enterprise architect who creates an enterprise-wide information systems infrastructure architecture for exiting systems and future systems to support business operations, business growth, and cooperation & collaboration with external parties.

Wood (2012) suggests similar view by arguing that chief information officers in the 21st century must be both technology and business experts and must be able to link technology with competitive business benefits, and he further proposes a number of questions to be asked when organizations are looking for or looking at their chief information officers:

- Can CIO directly correlate business value against information systems spend?
- Dose CIO know how your firm's information systems spend compares with that of competitors?
- Is information system function/operation a cost effective business partner?
- Can information systems promises be trusted in terms of it will deliver what it promise?
- Can security and risk issues be properly managed?
- Is there a clear strategy and path for de-commissioning old technology?
- Does CIO know technologies for business growth and competitive advantages?

- Do and How can we have the right and sufficient information systems talent in the organization?

In fact, chief information officer, who represents the information systems part of the organization, has to be a member of the organization's senior executive team and must have a say to the development of business strategy and to the strategic allocation of organizational resources, otherwise it is very difficult for information systems function/operation to effectively present business cases for information systems investments, to have effective input into the organization's strategic planning process, and to have full demonstration of the benefits and impacts of information systems projects/investments to the organization (especially the bottom line of the organization).

Chief information officers also could develop a technology road map for the whole organization, which looks at establishing a development path for making information systems more strategic (of course with good contribution from business side). Some aspects when they are developing a technology road map include (Alvarez & Raghavan 2010):

- Good understanding of business operations and value creation of the business.
- Good understanding of business needs regarding required information systems capabilities.
- Good evidence-based demonstration of return on information systems investment
- Good evidence-based demonstration of the contribution of information systems capabilities to business strategy
- Clear understanding of the gap between the current information sysetms status and required new information systems capabilities for business operations and business growth.
- Assurance of a joint effort between business and information systems when developing a technology road map. information
- Agreement on using the developed technology road map for capital and resource allocation decisions.
- Assurance to have the road map followed via governance mechanism.
- Good skills and knowledge in evaluating information systems strategic initiatives.
- Good understanding of the need for consistently refreshing the road map and updating the architecture as well as upgrading systems as needed.

On the other hand, people like Charlie Feld, former CIO of Frito-Lay and a great IS/IT leader argue (cited in Cooke & Baker 2011) that Chief Integration Officer could be a more appropriate title than Chief Information Officer since the important skills for today's information systems leaders should be system thinking skills: the ability to see the system (that is the company), identify dynamic patterns, and build information systems infrastructure and applications which are dynamic, relevant, and connected to the larger ecosystem including your organization's employees, customers, suppliers, partners and other relevant parties. They also suggest information systems leaders should be versatile, multidisciplinary and multicultural; and they should be responsible for creating a culture/environment in which people are working for the common goal, and team-works & peer relationships (i.e., most people do well because they don't hurt their relations with peers and let other team members down) are really encouraged. They further point out that the performance of leaders including information systems executives should be reviewed by taking into consideration of how they lead, manage, and develop people.

10.1.4 *Role of information systems in mergers and acquisitions*

Mergers and Acquisitions have been often used for the purposes of growth, market dominance, entering into new sectors/industries/markets and new areas/regions/countries, and acquiring required expertise and knowledge. Information systems can play an important role in mergers and acquisitions. As organizations increasingly rely on information systems for their operation, growth and competitive advantages, the problems in information systems in the mergers and acquisitions could be very costly. Sarrazin and West (2012, p. 34) state that "Many mergers don't live up to expectations, because they stumble on the integration of technology and operations". They also point out more than 50% of the synergies and integration in a merger are strongly associated with information systems. Some examples are: lowering information systems infrastructure costs, reducing information systems human resources costs, information systems procurement cost savings, integration of functional systems, and synchronizing data from different sources.

In order to play an effective role in the mergers and acquisitions, information systems operation/function has to be a part of the team from the very beginning. They should be an active player during the due intelligence process to identify information systems issues and insufficiencies as well as potential risks and liabilities in the target company by examining perspectives of applications and technology, information systems infrastructure, information systems skills & talent management, outsourcing activities, information systems demand management, and information systems operation/function management & governance. And hard decisions of which systems need to be maintained and integrated and which systems should be ceased have to be made once the scanning of IS/IT in the target company has been completed. Meanwhile if the acquiring firms' IS/IT infrastructure is flexible, scalable and adaptable, then integration in the mergers and acquisitions would become a much less issue.

10.1.5 *Recovering information systems in a disaster*

One unusual perspective of information systems operation management is recovering information systems in a disaster. Without careful preparation for unexpected disasters (i.e., hurricanes, earthquakes, floods, and other natural disasters), information systems operations will be seriously damaged or completely destroyed. One recent example of Hurricane Katrina (reported in Junglas & Ives 2007), which happened in the U.S. in 2009 and caused serious damage to information systems infrastructure of affected areas, has taught us lessons: (1) keeping data and data centers away from locations threatened by potential disasters; (2) Not assuming the public infrastructure will be available; (3) planning for civil unrest; (4) assuming some employees/people will not be available; (5) working with your suppliers on implementing a contingency and recovery plan; (6) expecting the unexpected; (7) being prepared for unexpected; (8) having a strong leadership position as a part of contingency and recovery plan; (9) empowering decision making in the uncertainty and disastrous situation, in which needs quick responses based on the circumstance and prior arrangements and pre-established decision hierarchies will not be followed; and (10) working on opportunities arising from the disasters (i.e., developing better and more advanced infrastructure to replace damaged and legacy infrastructure).

10.2 Outsourcing

Outsourcing is "an arrangement by which one organization provides a service or services for another organization that chooses not to perform them in-house" (Haag, Baltzan & Phillips 2008, p. 444). The business benefit of outsourcing is that an organisation can focus on its core competencies or core strengths, which allows an outsourcing provider to take over all non-core competencies. When organisations look at outsourcing as their choice, they face the choices of in-sourcing, outsourcing and offshore outsourcing. Each of these has its own advantages and disadvantages (Haag, Baltzan & Phillips 2006, pp. 157–160, pp. 290–293) (see Table 10.1). A systematic, balanced and integrated decision-making approach, taking into consideration various issues (i.e. costs, benefits), should be followed.

Table 10.1: Comparison of in-sourcing, outsourcing and offshore outsourcing of systems development

Systems Development	Advantages	Disadvantages
In-sourcing	Improves requirements determination Increases knowledge worker participation and ownership Increases speed of systems development	Inadequate knowledge worker expertise leads to inadequately developed systems Lack of organizational focus creates "privatized" systems Insufficient analysis of design alternatives leads to sub-par systems Lack of documentation and external support leads to short-lived systems

Continued on next page

Table 10.1 – continued from previous page

Systems Development	Advantages	Disadvantages
Outsourcing	Focuses on unique core competencies. And outsourcing non-core processes allows businesses to focus on their core competencies Exploits the intellect of another organization Better predict future costs Acquires leading-edge technology Reduces costs, i.e. reduced operating expenses Improves performance accountability Increases quality and efficiency Reduces exposure to risk Access to outsourcing service providers economies of scale and expertise and best-in-class practices	Reduces technical know-how for future innovation Reduces degree of control Increases vulnerability of strategic information Increases dependency on other organizations
Offshore Outsourcing	Could realize saving of 30%–50% Attainment of higher service levels Freeing up of in-house management to focus on strategic management as opposed to daily operational issues	Unproven on large scales Instability of the offshore countries Language, culture, and time zone issues Reduced degree of control

(Source: Developed from Haag, Baltzan & Phillips 2006, pp. 157–160, 290–293)

Leading offshore outsourcing countries include Canada, India, Ireland, Israel, and the Philippines while up-and-coming offshore outsourcing countries include Brazil, China, Malaysia, Mexico, Russia, and South Africa. Argentina, Chile, Costa Rica, New Zealand,

Thailand, and the Ukraine are some rookie offshore outsourcing countries (Haag, Baltzan & Phillips 2008, pp. 447–453).

While enjoying some benefits of outsourcing, organisations also face challenges. Some challenges of outsourcing identified by Haag, Baltzan and Phillips (2008, pp. 453–454) include: contract length (most outsourcing contracts span several years), competitive edge (loss of competitive advantage resulting from loss of effective and innovative use of information systems), information confidentiality issues, and problems in defining scope.

However organisations can avoid the risks by considering some of the following activities suggested by Pearlson and Saunders (2010, p. 197):

- Do not negotiate solely on price.
- Develop full life cycle service contracts that occur in stages.
- Establish short-term supplier contracts.
- Hire multiple, best-of-breed suppliers.
- Build up skills in contract management.
- Thoroughly assess outsourcers' capabilities.
- Select an outsourcer whose applications complement yours.
- Make a choice on cultural fit as well as technical expertise.
- Examine whether a particular outsourcing relationship produces a net benefit for your company.
- Plan transition to offshoring
- Use SOAs to increase agility

10.2.1 *Critical capabilities for offshore outsourcing of information systems*

By studying 18 firms, Ranganathan and Balaji (2007) identify four major outsourcing capabilities: (1) systemic thinking on offshore outsourcing (capability to strategize and offshore readiness); (2) global information systems vendor management (vendor selection, contract facilitation and relationship governance); (3) global information systems resource management (human resource management, knowledge management and distributed work management); and (4) information systems change management (managing user-related change and dealing with organizational change). They also put forward five lessons learned/suggestions for effective offshore outsourcing management: (1) taking a systematic approach to developing offshore outsourcing capabilities; (2) working on the entire outsourcing lifecycle; (3) acknowledging the dynamic nature of capabilities; (4) investing in structure and people; and (5) regularly auditing offshore outsourcing capabilities.

10.3 Global Information Systems Operation Management

With the assistance of information technology, many companies throughout the world are attempting to transform themselves into global players (O'Brien & Marakas 2011, p. 598). The changes in the marketplace, the rapid adoption of the Internet and development of Internet technologies have presented organisations with new opportunities (i.e. reaching global customers, establishing global supply chains) and challenges (i.e. political, cultural, geo-economic challenges). The management issues are enormous and need to be carefully evaluated if organisations wish to reap the full benefits of the global market. Like any other business operations an essential part of global information systems management is to explore the impacts of cultural, political and geo-economic realties in different business locations. In addition, organisations also need to pay a lot of attention to such issues as establishing global business information systems strategies, managing global business application portfolios, building global information systems platforms, dealing with global data resources, and working on global systems development (O'Brien & Marakas 2011, pp. 601).

One area needing particular attention is cross-border data access and transmission since cross-border data flows may be viewed as violating a nation's sovereignty for the reason it avoids customs duties and regulations. Other issues concerning cross-border data communication include: laws protecting the local information systems industry from competition, laws protecting local jobs, and privacy legislations. Some key issues of cross-border data communication include (O'Brien & Marakas 2011, p. 606): (1) networking management issues (i.e., operational efficiency of networks, data communication security issues); (2) regulatory issues (i.e., cross-border data flow restrictions, international communication regulations, international politics); (3) technology issues (i.e., network infrastructure across countries, international integration of technologies, applications, systems); and (4) country-oriented issues (i.e., national differences and characteristics, international tariff structures).

Information systems can play an important role in developing a faster, more agile, and innovative global organization. To effectively and efficiently support global operations, organizations need to take a combined approach of decentralization (to look after local information systems needs and unique requirements and skills) and centralization (to leverage the scale of information systems globally and take advantages of the power of centralized computing (i.e., best of breed and standardized technologies, common platforms, and shared services for application development and infrastructure for the sake of efficiency and cost saving).

One good example of such approach is Ford's information system transformation in recent years, with evidence of Ford's latest SUNC and my Ford Touch innovations. By applying centralized federated information systems management model (Ford's name for the combined approach), Ford has simplified, centralized and delivered information systems as a service across its globe operations while allowing sufficient room for localization and customization (Dignan 2012; Hiner 2012). The drive behind this is Ford's emphasis on new product developments and sales: any information systems initiatives are not contributing to these goals will not be approved or will be stopped. In addition, Ford's information systems operation has been focused on four priorities: integrating applications, supporting growth, enabling collaboration, and improving internal efficiency. One particular point of integration is integrating BYOD (bring-your-own-devices) into the corporate computing infrastructure in line with the popularity of mobile computing and enterprise mobility. When implementing the combined approach at the local level, the buying and cooperation of local leadership is very critical. Local leaders have to be included in the process and be consulted, and benefits of the implementation (especially to the local operations) and the impacts of not-implementing (especially to the local operations) should be clearly communicated to local leaders. Otherwise they will feel the threat (that headquarter will have more control) and don't have the feeling of ownership.

In addition, Benni, Muto and Wang (2011) suggest three essential management skills for implementing global enterprise resource planning projects, which are generic in nature, could be applied to other global information systems projects. The three suggested essential management skills are:

- Setting and steering company-wide priorities to define the target operating model of the global project: including activities such as developing priorities with management and other stakeholders via workshops; agreeing on the level of consolidation, standardization, and automation needed to align with identified priorities; and establishing project teams with commitments and tangible support from top management to clear the potential political hurdles.
- Translating the target operating model into an information systems architecture: including activities such as developing an architecture as per the agree target operating model with the room for localization and customization, aligning and ensuring the expected business outcomes with the suggested architecture, and adjusting information systems operation/function (internal organizational changes within information systems operation/function) to be ready for the transition to the target operating model.

- Fine-tuning change management approach: including activities such as clearly communicating every aspect of forthcoming changes, i.e., when, why, how the changes are going to happen?, what is expected from people?, and who will be change champions?; refining and reinforcing change management processes; assigning task forces to drive changes; and emphasizing the change management is focusing on business transformation (so communication and negotiation are critical) rather than basic information systems implementation.

10.3.1 *Managing global virtual teams*

Global virtual software development teams have often been used by organizations to utilize firm's global-wide in-house expertise, but the lack of face-to-face interactions has made working together virtually a not easy task. Siebdrat, Hoegl and Ernst (2009) argue virtual collaboration has to be managed in specific ways and provide some suggestions based on their studies of 80 software development teams from 28 labs worldwide:

- Emphasizing social and teamwork skills: team members from different cultures and different functions have to be able to effectively communicate and work together. When forming global teams, organizations can not solely look at candidates' expertise and availability, but also social and teamwork skills.
- Promoting self-leadership and developing self-sufficiency: experienced team leaders should be assigned to the global team whenever possible and sufficient training should be given team members to ensure each team member could contribute fully and complete their assigned tasks by overcoming geographic dispersion and cultural diversity issues on his/her own.
- Providing face-to-face meetings: A project kick-off face-to-face meeting or/and social gathering before the project starts is necessary for establishing a common ground in the beginning of the project. Of course periodic face-to-face meetings will be better.
- Fostering a global mind-set: every team member should see him/her as a part of international networks, and recognize the international nature of the organization. Approaches for developing global mind-set include short-term international assignments at overseas locations of the organization and inter-cultural training.

10.4 Summary

Information systems can play a very important role in the success of organisation's competitive strategies. However competitive strategies alone cannot create magic. The success of such strategies heavily relies on good information systems management. In this chapter, three important aspects of information systems management, namely enterprise information systems operation, global information systems operation, and outsourcing were discussed.

Bibliography

Agarwal, R., Brown, C. V., Ferratt, T. W. & Moore, J. E. 2006, 'Five mindsets for retaining IT staff', *MIS Quarterly Executive*, Vol. 5, No. 3, pp. 137–150.

Alvarez, E. & Raghavan, S. 2010, 'Road Map to Relevance: How a capabilities-driven information technology strategy can help differentiate your company', *Strategy + Business*, Iss. 61, pp. 1–6.

Applegate, L. M., Austin, R. D. & Soule, D. L. 2009, *Corporate Information Strategy and Management: Text and Cases*, 8th Edition, McGraw-Hill, USA.

Benni, E., Muto, K. & Wang, K. W. 2011, 'Tailoring IT to global operations', *McKinsey on Business Technology*, Number 24, pp. 2–7.

Bensemhoun, D., Chartrin, C. & Kropf, M. 2011, 'Tracking the roots of underperformance in banks' IT', *McKinsey on Business Technology*, Number 24, pp. 22–27.

Boochever, J. O., Park, T. & Weinberg, J. C. 2002, 'CEO vs CIO: Can this marriage be saved', *Strategy + Business*, Iss.28, pp. 1–10.

Booth, A., Roberts, R. & Sikes, J. 2011, 'How strong is your IT strategy?', *McKinsey on Business Technology*, Number 23, Summer 2011, pp. 2–7.

Chartrin, C. 2011, 'Brining learn to a Skilled workforce: An interview with Thierry Pécoud of BNP Paribas', *McKinsey on Business Technology*, Number 24, pp. 28–31.

Chui, M. & Fleming, T. 2011, 'Inside P & G's digital revolution', *McKinsey Quarterly*, November 2011, pp. 1-11.

Cooker, M. & Baker, E. 2010, 'Helping the CIO lead', *Strategy + Business*, December 13, 2010, Online Available at: http://www.strategy-business.com/article/00055?gko=ebedc (accessed Aug 2, 2012).

Copper, B. & Nocket, K. 2009, 'Toyota's IT Transformation', *Strategy + Business*, Iss.55, pp. 1–3.

Dignan, L. 2012, *Four IT management lessons from Ford*, Online Available at: http://www.zdnet.com/four-it-management-lessons-from-ford-7000000520/ (accessed July 20, 2012).

Fred, C. S. & Stoddard, D. B. 2004, 'Getting IT right', *Harvard Business Review*, February 2004, pp. 72–79.

Haag, S., Baltzan, p. & Phillips, A. 2006, *Business Driven Technology*, 1st edition, McGraw-Hill Irwin, Boston, USA.

Haag, S., Baltzan, p. & Phillips, A. 2008, *Business Driven Technology*, 2nd edition, McGraw-Hill Irwin, Boston, USA.

Hiner, J. 2012, *How Ford Reimagined IT from the Inside-out to Power its Turnaround*, Online Available at: http://www.techrepublic.com/blog/hiner/how-ford-reimagined-it-from-the-inside-out-to-power-its-turnaround/10671 (accessed August 2, 2012).

IDG Connect 2011, *IDG Connect Special Report: The Global IT Skills Landscape*, Summer 2011, IDG Connect International, pp. 1–8.

Junglas, I. & Ives, B. 2007, 'Recovering IT in a disaster: Lessons from Hurricane Katrina', *MIS Quarterly Executive*, Vol. 6, No. 1, pp. 39–51.

Manyika, J. 2009, 'Hal Varian on how the Web challenges managers", *McKinsey Quarterly*, January 2009, On-line available at: https://www.mckinseyquarterly.com/Strategy/Innovation/Hal_Varian_on_how_the_Web_challenges_managers_2286 (accessed July 23, 2012).

O'Brien, J. A. & Marakas, G. M. 2011, *Management Information Systems*, 10th Edition, McGraw-Hill, New York, USA.

Pearlson, K. E. & Saunders, C. S. 2010, *Managing and Using Information Systems: A Strategic Approach*, Fourth Edition, John Wiley & Sons, USA.

Ranganathan, C. & Balaji, S. 2007, 'Critical capabilities for offshore outsourcing of information systems', *MIS Quarterly Executive*, Vol. 6, No. 3, pp. 147–164.

Roberts, R. Sarrazin, H. & Sikes, J. 2010, 'Reshaping IT management for turbulent times', *McKinsey on Business Technology*, Number 21, pp. 2–9.

Sarrazin, H. & West, A. 2010, 'Understanding the strategic value of IT in M&A', *McKinsey on Business Technology*, Number 21, pp. 34–39.

Siebdrat, F., Hoegl, M. & Ernst, H. 2010, 'How to manage virtual teams', *MIT Sloan Management Review*, Vol. 50, No.4., pp. 63–69.

Weill, p. 2004, *Don't just lead, govern: How top-performing firms govern IT*, Working Paper No, 341, Center for Information Systems Research, Sloan School of Management, Massachusetts Institute of Technology, pp. 1–21.

Wood, D. 2012, 'Does you CIO have what it takes', *Forbes*, 05072012, Online Available at: www.forbes.com/sites/danwoods/20120705/does-your-cio-have-what-it-takes/print/ (accessed July 9, 2012).

The manufacturer's authorised representative in the EU is Springer Nature Customer Service Centre GmbH, Europaplatz 3, 69115 Heidelberg, Germany. If you have any concerns regarding our products, please contact ProductSafety@springernature.com

Printed and bound by CPI Group (UK) Ltd, Croydon, CR0 4YY

25/03/2026

02078174-0019